RICHARD M. JONES

THE GREAT GALE

GALE

∽∽ OF 1871 ∽∽

RICHARD M. JONES

THE GREAT GALE

OF 1871

MEREO
Cirencester

Published by Mereo

Mereo is an imprint of Memoirs Publishing

1A The Wool Market Cirencester Gloucestershire GL7 2PR
Tel: 01285 640485, Email: info@mereobooks.com
www.memoirspublishing.com, www.mereobooks.com

Republished in England, October 2013

Book jacket design Ray Lipscombe

ISBN 978-1-909544-72-7

Printed in England

Contents

Prologue

Preface

Prologue

On Christmas Day morning 2004, just after Midnight Mass at Bridlington Priory, librarian Sarah Stocks sat at a friend's house having drinks when a local man came over to her and asked her out of the blue if the library had copies of the *Yorkshire Post* from years gone by. Her reply was that the library kept current newspapers for a maximum of one year and wondered "Why did you ask?"

The man, who owns Marton Grange Hotel on the road to Flamborough, was carrying out a major renovation to his hotel, and when the skirting board was pulled apart, they found an old *Yorkshire Post* filling a hole in the wall. It had been stuffed there by the owners at the time as there was obviously a draught, a very big draught, caused by severe weather and gales. The best thing to do at that time would have been to grab an old newspaper, maybe yesterday's newspaper once everyone had finished reading it, and stuff the hole. The date on the paper was 9th February 1871.

And there had indeed been a tremendous draught, and a great gale. This is the story of that gale.

The Yorkshire Post of 9th February 1871.

Preface

On 9th February 1861 a storm occurred on the North Yorkshire coast that shook the town of Whitby. Several ships were sunk but all the crews were saved. It was the heroism of the lifeboat crew that has captured the imagination since. The 13 lifeboat crew put out to sea despite the fact that the previous rescues had left them hungry and exhausted. It really had been a non-stop, but winning, battle. By 2pm that day the schooner Merchant was in the stages of running onto the beach and the lifeboat began pulling alongside the vessel. But at that moment the boat was turned completely over, throwing her crew into the sea. The struggling crew were only around 50 yards from the pier and wearing lifejackets, but only one of these men, Henry Freeman, would make it to shore. Of the 13 men who set out for the daring rescue, he was the sole survivor. The people lining the shores to see the drama unfold were horrified, but could do nothing except watch. Rockets were fired to aid the men, and several onlookers dived in to save the men only to find them- selves in need of help. But all their efforts were futile, and there was no hope for the crew. They left a total of 46 children father- less, and ten wives as widows.

Freeman would continue to be a lifeboatman for a further 40 years until he died at the age of 69 on 13th December 1904, having served a lifetime on the sea, spending 22 years as coxswain of Whitby lifeboat and helping to save a total of over 300 lives. This is etched on his gravestone today.

It is with tragic irony that ten years and one day later, exactly the same tragedy would happen just down the coast, but with a staggering death toll which would shake a small Yorkshire town just like Whitby.

Chapter 1

Calm before the storm

The year 1871 started off peaceful and uneventful. Amadeus I became king of Spain on 2nd January. The Franco-Prussian war ended with the surrender of France, just over a week later. And for the people of the small Yorkshire town of Bridlington, it was hopefully going to be a good year for the fishing industry.

The town was split into two parts: the town of Bridlington was centred around the 700-year-old Priory Church, whereas the fishing community was living in the part known as Bridlington Quay, centred around the fishing harbour which for centuries had been the be all and end all of the Quay's income. Most of the people, if they weren't fishermen, were farmers, labourers, joiners, and most of them fended for themselves in order to feed their families. The harbour itself was crammed with small boats, some manned by only one, maybe two, people, who risked life and limb going out in the next available good weather to catch a few measly fish or crabs.

Sometimes a boat would go out and return the same evening with a successful haul that would feed a family for days to come. But in this game you had to take the rough with the smooth and some days you could come back with virtually nothing, certain- ly not worth going out for, but it was a risk they had to take, which they did time and time again. In an era which saw no motor cars, electricity, gas central heating, production lines, it must have been very hard for these people to live compared with nowadays.

Down on the harbour sat one of these boats. A working boat as well as a lifeboat, the *Harbinger* hung from the harbour wall covered in a tarpaulin, ready and waiting should it be needed in an emergency launch using the davits. She was privately owned and run by the locals of Bridlington, who felt it necessary to have a second lifeboat. However funding was not at its best on schemes of this nature, so it had been paid for and donated by a man named Count Gustav Batthyany, a friend to many of the town's fishermen, who loved the Yorkshire coast, especially Bridlington. An Austro-Hungarian, he lived in Bridlington until moving to Grove Cottage, 1 Eastgate South, Driffield, with eight servants in 1872 (and later No 1 Belmont Road, Scarborough) and he made regular visits to Bridlington. Born in Vienna, Austria, he was 42 years old, and had come to Britain due to troubles in his homeland, thinking it safer to reside in England for the time being. His father, the prime minister of Hungary, was caught in the uprising against the Austria/Hungary empire and was tried, convicted and executed. In the count's opinion it would be a while, if at all, before he would travel back to his homeland.

The lifeboat paid for by Batthyany was built by local joiner David Purdon in his yard at No 4 North Street, behind the Central Methodist Church. Smaller than the town's main lifeboat *Robert Whitworth*, and much lighter than the RNLI boat, she was given to the local fishermen by the Count in 1863. Made of mahogany, she was christened in the afternoon of 1st January 1866 and was put to the test for the first time in company with a crowd of spectators (ironically from Trinity Cut, the place where she would make her first launch in the Great Gale). She was then taken into the harbour where the crew did the capsize test, getting freezing cold and soaking wet, but proving the boat could right herself with no problems. She was then flooded with water, and emptied by taking out three of the four plugs in less than half a minute. It was decided her resting place would be on the harbour wall for easiness of launch.

She was 27 feet long and had a beam of 6ft. 3in. She had eight oars and carried a crew of nine.

But Bridlington had two lifeboats. *Harbinger* was privately owned but the RNLI had also a boat, which was the *Robert Whitworth*. This was known as the "Institute boat" whereas the *Harbinger* was the "fishermen's boat." Nevertheless they were both crewed by willing volunteers. So many in fact that a lot of the time they had to be turned away because too many had turned up!

In 1866 Bridlington received a new RNLI boat, which keeps the name of the old boat, *Robert Whitworth*, the design being different, even though the boat they were replacing was only a year old. The *Robert Whitworth (II)* was a gift from the Manchester branch, named after Mr Robert Whitworth, and owned by the RNLI. She was 32ft. long and had ten oars. She was housed at the end of Chapel Street (now H. Samuels jewellers).

On the harbour was the office of the harbourmaster, who in 1871 was John Campleman. His office looked over the harbour into the bay. A quiet still stretch of water, Bridlington Bay was known by sailors as the "Bay of Safety" due to the sandbanks and cliffs offering a natural reprieve from fierce storms and heavy seas, and also a good place to anchor if they got into difficulty.

The town of Bridlington was a small fishing town split into two, with Bridlington centred round the ancient Priory Church, and Bridlington Quay centred around the harbour. But a small town does not necessarily mean small people. For an unlikely band of heroes was to emerge in the gale of 1871. Normal every- day people, fishermen, scholars, tailors, policemen, they would very soon be the talk of the town for many years to come.

One of these was David Purdon, aged 38. He was born in Skipsea in 1832 to David Purdon Snr and Sarah Habbershaw. He was a joiner and cabinet maker. He was very skilled in building boats, and was tasked with constructing the *Harbinger* in 1865. He and his wife Hannah, whom he married in Hull in June 1857, had a daughter Sarah Jane, baptised at Bridlington Quay on 5th September 1858. They lived together on Chapel Street, where David employed two people in his business as a joiner. Hannah died at the age of 28 on 3rd July 1861.

Harriet Wilson (born in Ellerker on 24th March 1842) became David's second wife on 2nd September 1862, in a ceremony at the Parish Church, Scarborough. She was pregnant with their fourth child at the time of the Gale. They already had Anne (born 9th August 1864, baptised 6th September 1864), Frederick George (born 1865, baptised 18th June 1865) and Sarah Jane and Isabel (born 19th February 1869). He lived at 15 King Street. He was on the general committee of the Sailors' and Working Men's Club from 1867 to 1869.

Purdon had taken over the North Street yard and business from a Mr R. Smith, who had died, and Purdon began work in January 1868. He also had another workshop between the Quay Methodist Chapel and Princess Street.

John Robinson had gained his master's certificate and he took command of the schooner *Queen Dowager* in 1843, which was the last ship to be built in Bridlington, two years earlier. Sailing from all the major ports in Britain like London and Liverpool,

Robinson's seafaring took him to all corners of the globe. He had also served on the second-to-last ship built in Bridlington, the *Queen*, in 1842, as a mate. It was when he was struck down with a bad case of sunstroke, that he had to abandon his life at sea and resort to being a fisherman in his home town. This he was happy enough with. As well as being in the lifeboat on every occasion possible, John Robinson had been coxswain of the *Harbinger* for two years.

William Cobb, a single man, had just recently completed his apprenticeship as a Navigating Officer at sea and was in Bridlington to visit his parents before settling down to study for his second mate's certificate. He was staying at 11 North Street, where his father Francis lived as a mariner.

Forty-three-year-old James Watson had married Eliza Willis on 25th November 1862 at Christ Church, Bridlington Quay, conducted by minister Mortimer Tylor, with Thomas Holiday Willis and Rebecca Willis as witnesses. The son of a mariner (John Watson), he was 34 while his bride, the daughter of Francis Willis (a blacksmith), was just 23. She had lived in Reighton all her life up until this point. In 1861 he lived on Chapel Street with his mother Jane Watson and his son Thomas.

Richard Atkin, 45, had a wife, Margaret, and five children, and lived his life in Bridlington as a fisherman. John Snarr Clappison, 21, a resident of the village of Sigglesthorne, was hired by Purdon as a joiner.

Robert Pickering, 34, lived at 1 Chapel Street, Bridlington, and was a mariner. He had been brought up only a few doors down at his parents at number 19 (now a jewellers). His father was also called Robert. Robert Jnr married Elizabeth Pant in 1868, despite the fact she had two illegitimate children, one being born just a few months before they were married. In 1871 she was 25 years old, with her two children John, seven, and Frederick Pant.

Robert Hopper lived at 26 Grundell Terrace with his wife Annie and daughters Margaret, Kate, Mary, and sons Tom, Harry, John and George. He was born in Chapel Street. He had been at sea since aged 12 when he was sailing out of Bridlington on the schooner *Acheen*, of which his father Captain W. Hopper was master. He was then apprenticed as a sail-maker before going back to sea. On his return he married Annie. He again took to the sea aboard the schooner *Twin Sisters*, before going back on the *Acheen* as mate in 1857, and even took charge of the ship in his father's absence. However an incident where the ship nearly grounded near the south pier caused him to stick to sail- making in Filey, returning to Bridlington to be a fisherman when the weather was good, and a sail-maker in winter. He owned the coble *Hilda*. He took part in sailing races in the Bridlington Regatta of August 1869 with David Purdon, winning third and second places in two of the races.

Richard Bedlington lived at 30 Queen Street with

his wife Susannah, his daughters Elizabeth, Eliza, Laura, and his son Joseph Richard. One of ten siblings, he was the only male.

After bad weather had delayed sailing, hundreds of ships were waiting to make the journey from the Tyne and Tees down the east coast of Yorkshire bound for the south, some going to London, others farther afield to such as Paris where there was a short supply of much-needed coal due to the siege. As the ships lay alongside the docks, they were loaded to the brim with coal, hoping for a break in the bad weather. When this came, it made the captains realise that the time had come to sail while the going was good, and that they may not get another chance for a while. With calm seas and full ships, most of which were carry- ing coal, the huge fleet of up to 400 ships sailed and headed out to sea. However, these ships were overloaded by the selfish owners who thought nothing of sending rotting, leaking ships to sea with too much cargo. If they made it to their destination, then all was well. If they were lost at sea, the insurers would pay out. In those days it was common practice to send a ship to sea so overloaded that in some cases the water would lap over the main deck . . . and that would be in a flat calm! To make matters worse, nearly all of these ships were in a very bad state of repair, rotting, leaking, some barely seaworthy. One, the *Friends Increase*, was 69 years old at the time she was wrecked in the Gale.

This angered the Derby MP Samuel Plimsoll, who for several years had campaigned without success to make it law to have a safe load line drawn at the bow of every vessel close to the waterline.

The next day, 10th February, would be his 47th birthday. But what was to happen would not give anyone a cause for celebration. The fleet of ships had been hugging the coast in case of storm so they could shelter as soon as they could, but arriving off Flamborough Head on the evening of 9th February, the winds died down and forced many of the ships to anchor in the Bay until the conditions were right to continue. Off Bridlington was now a huge fleet of small ships, with crews waiting for a favourable wind.

The Scarborough fishing smack *Vivid*, under Captain Vary, sailed on the afternoon of Thursday, 9th February. Vary had sailed for 30 years without incident and had no reason to believe that this voyage was going to be any different. He carried a crew of three.

The *Arrow*, a brig from the port of Sunderland, sailed loaded with coal on Thursday night bound for London. She was owned by Mr Philip Stubbs and was 26 years old, had recently under- gone extensive repairs but was not insured. Her five crew were under the command of Captain Robson on this Sunderland to London trip loaded with coal. At 176 tons, she had a supple- mentary trysail mast.

The schooner/brigantine *Caroline* of Yarmouth was on a voyage from Blyth to Caen (France) with coal under the com- mand of Captain Carter and four crew. She was built in Yarmouth in 1839 and owned by Garson Blake.

The Lynn brigantine *Peri*, under command of Captain Charles Cook, was taking their complement of coal and five crew from Seaham back to Lynn. She had been built in Newcastle in 1845 and her tonnage registered at 126. Her owner was a W. Watson. Captain Cook lived at 13 Mill Fleet Terrace, Lynn.

The schooner *Margaret* of Ipswich was bound from Seaham to Ipswich with five crew, led by Captain William Howard, who was also the owner. She had been built in Deptford in 1844 with a tonnage of 104, and was carrying a cargo of coal.

The brig *Delta*, of Whitby, was built in Sunderland in 1839 and her registered tonnage was 226. Owned by 64-year-old Thomas Forrest, she was heading down the coast with Captain William Calvert and his four crew with a cargo of coal. This vessel would play one of the most tragic roles in the story of the Great Gale.

The brig *Echo* of Maldon was 58 years old when she sailed from Sunderland bound for Rochester with coal. Under the command of Captain Davenish, she had a further five crew.

The schooner *Bebside* belonged to Mr Edward Mackenzie of Blyth, registered at 103 tons. Built in 1841, she was carrying a cargo of oak from Blyth to Trouville (at the entrance to the Seine, France) under the command of Captain Sellers and his three crew.

The *Friends Increase* was a staggering 69-year-old barque from London bound for Newcastle. Her cargo of oak timber was in the hands of Captain Tabor and his three crew. Her tonnage was registered at 74 and she was owned by William Olley. (These days ships like this would not even be allowed to sail. She must have been in poor condition at that age!). She was built at Mistley in Essex on the River Stour by Jancey Betts as a 122- ton cutter.

The *Spinner* was the property of Mr John Dixon of Blyth and was registered at 173 tons.

The brig *Agility* was owned by Mr Thomas Ord of North Shields, registered at 180 tons. On this voyage from Shields to London, she was under the command of Captain Pringle and his five crew with a cargo of coal.

The *Lavinia* sailed from Seaham harbour on the ninth loaded with 240 tons of coal bound for Portsmouth. Registered at 144 tons, she was only partly insured. She carried a captain, Anthony Hindson, and three crew. Owned by William Watson, she was built in 1825 in Lynn.

The *Rebecca and Elizabeth*, a wooden two-masted schooner, was en route from Hartlepool to Wisbech with coal. At 61ft. 6in. long, with a beam of 18ft. 7in. and a draught of 7ft. 8in., she was just 59.99 tons. Built in 1845 in Merionethshire, Wales, she was owned by W. Kirk and W. Withers of Lowestoft. She had been registered in Hartlepool until 1863. She was carrying coal under the command of Captain Dutton and his three crew.

The *Teresita*, built in 1854 at New Brunswick and registered at Harwich, was a square stern brig with one deck and two masts, with a gross tonnage of 134.6. The owner was John Henry Vaux, a well-known figure in Harwich being Lord Mayor in the 1870s.

The vessel was 82.7ft. long, 22.3ft. wide and a depth of 12.1ft., and her bow was adorned with a female bust figurehead until it was removed in 1855. Vaux had been her owner for only 13 months, buying the vessel from Hannah Cole, who had had it left to her after her husband Daniel had died in August 1856.

The *Produce*, owned by her master Captain William Flisher, was sailing bound for Folkestone with coal. A seaman named George Wade left at Shields and "a coloured man whose name is unknown" took his place. An apprentice also jumped ship at the same port so the vessel was a man down for this voyage. So with a complement of six, she headed down the coast. Regis- tered at 177 tons, she had been built in Berwick in 1834.

The Shields brig *Spinney* was bound Boulogne to Blyth in ballast.

The Whitstable sloop *John* was sailing to Scotland with a cargo of potatoes with her master, 45-year-old Captain Steed Laraman, and two crew, brothers Henry and John Coleman, aged 16 and 18 respectively. The ship was owned by a Mr Holmes of Herne Bay and was known locally as the "old John" because of her age. Steed was married to Mary Ann, a greengrocer, and lived at 50 Harbour Street, Whitstable, and had four children, Emily (18), Sydney (8), Adeline (5) and Minnie A. (1).

The two brothers had lost their father James Pearson Coleman, also a mariner, and they were the men of the house, earning a living for their mother and younger siblings.

The *Rapid* was a square brig built in Aberdeen in 1834. Under the ownership of Isaac Bedlington & Co., she was carrying a cargo of iron and a crew of six under the command of Captain Hutchinson. She was based in Whitby.

The Whitby brig *Squirrel* was built in Pictoll, Nova Scotia, in 1836 and was owned by Will Simpson. On this voyage from Seaham to Lowestoft, she carried coal and a crew of four, led by Captain Peek.

The *William Maitland* was a 32-year-old brig built in Aberdeen, owned by John H. Storm with a registered tonnage of

138. Her captain Anthony Newton and his five crew were taking the ship from Hartlepool to Chatham with coal.

The Shields brig *Windsor* was built in 1839 at Prince Edward Island, and was 192 tons. Captain Woodhouse and his five crew were bound from Shields to London with coal.

The *Worthy*, built in Sunderland in 1857, was a Lynn brig of 149 tons, owned by BC Bridges and commanded by Captain Frost. He and his five crew were going from Newcastle back to Lynn with coal.

The *Yare* was also from Lynn, owned by Thomas Spurr and built in 1837 in Yarmouth. She was a 23-ton smack with coal and two crew including Captain Heard, bound from Shields to Lynn.

Up the coast, ships were facing a similar situation but they didn't have the luxury of a bay of safety and many of them had to remain out at sea. Among them was the *Henry*, of Goole, which was sailing down to Portsmouth, owned by a Mr Shelcroft of London, and the *Terminus* of Blyth, which was said to be overloaded with coal (the official figures put it at "80 chaldron by bill of lading"). Her registered tonnage was 134 and she was a very old ship.

The scene was set for one of the biggest disasters ever to hit the east coast of England. Hundreds of ships were at anchor in the false hope that the Bay would provide the cover they would need. Little did they know that their bay of safety would ultimately lead to their demise. For as Friday morning, 10th February 1871, came, a change in the wind came too. A change that would mean disaster.

Chapter 2

DISASTER

Friday, 10th February, 1871

Bridlington has seen many a storm in its days. The winds come and go in a Jekyll and Hyde kind of way. Sometimes the weather can be calm, sunny and a pleasure for the thousands of people who turn up at the coast for the summer year after year. But quicker than can be imagined, the winds can turn nasty and for thousands more of the sailors caught up in it, it could be treacherous, deadly and dangerous. For hundreds of years too, ships have been coming to grief along these shores. The sharp jutting rocks of Flamborough Head show no mercy to any ship unlucky enough to go astray from the regular shipping channels, which in those days usually meant hugging the coast enough to provide a wind break but far enough away to avoid disaster. No-one knows for sure how many wrecks litter this short stretch of coastline.

Estimates today, after two world wars and several major storms, make the toll of ships in their thousands.

The most famous ship to be sunk here is the

Bonhomme Richard. She was an American warship which engaged a British convoy off Flamborough Head in 1779. After a ferocious battle lasting most of the night, Captain John Paul Jones of the *Richard* boarded the British warship *HMS Serapis* and watched his own ship sink. There the legend of John Paul Jones, now known as the father of the American navy, and the Battle of Flamborough Head was born. At the time of print, wreck hunters were still searching for this prize relic.

Also off this coast is *HMS Falcon*, sunk in the First World War. Her commanding officer was Charles Lightoller, the most senior surviving officer of the wreck of the *Titanic* in 1912.

All along the Yorkshire coast there are stories of wrecks, storms, survival, tragedy, sinking liners, warships, submarines, fishing vessels. The North Sea is a ship's graveyard and a huge history book waiting to be opened at the same time.

Then, on the morning of 10th February 1871, the east coast was to witness yet another chapter in its dark maritime history. For at around 2am the winds began to increase, just slightly at first. Then within an hour it was getting more noticeable, and steadily, gradually, as if the storm was coaxing itself to life, it was a full-blown gale by daybreak. The local townsfolk took shelter in their homes and people who were still caught up in it made headway to get under somewhere dry. The temperatures dropped and the air bit the hands and faces of the crews of the ships, who were running around their decks securing every-thing down, tying everything to the deck to stop it shifting. The biggest danger was a cargo shifting and the ship taking on a list. Should that happen, the ship would only go one way as there was no way in this weather it could be rectified. If anything on board could move, they had to make sure it didn't any more! At sea on a boat like this, the least little wave could rock everything from side to side, causing every object not secured down to fly uncontrollably across the cabin. Simple things like a cup or a plate can cause serious injury when it hits someone at lighting speed. Sailors learn quickly by their mistakes or they pay for it painfully!

The fleet of ships still at anchor was now being tossed about like toys in a bath. The crews were most likely becoming very restless, having no sleep, dodging flying objects; even standing upright would become a challenge to even the most experienced of the sailors. But nothing prepared them for what was about to come. The first casualties of the Great Gale had already happened just down the coast.

At Stony Binks, two miles to the east of Spurn, the schooner *Fortune Teller*, bound for Plymouth from Clackmullen under the command of Captain William Cundy, grounded on shore around midnight. The crew took to the rigging and burned lights which were seen on shore and a rescue operation swung into action. The local lifeboat was launched and soon reached the wreck to save the crew of four men, the captain and a boy. This ship came from Fowey, Cornwall, and was owned by a Mr John Henry Hooken. The survivors were safely on shore by 5.30am, when the exhausted and frozen men were revived by locals. The first wreck of the day turned out

Paintings by J. T. Allerston.

Firing the Very rocket over the *Saviour*.

to have a happy ending. They would be the lucky ones. After anchoring overnight in Bridlington Bay, the fleet of small wooden ships was now stuck where they lay, in between the cliffs of Flamborough, the Smithick Sands and Bridlington north beach. Due to the high winds being SSE, the Bay of Safety now became a death trap. There was no escape. Unless the wind dramatically changed, and fast, the men on the ships knew that many of these rickety old vessels would not survive the day. With so many ships in visible distress, it would have been hard for the townsfolk to wonder where to begin. But the nightmare had barely begun, for the ships began dragging their anchors across the seabed, and as dawn broke over the bay that morning, the first signs of distress of the terrified crews were seen.

It is unclear what happened on the shores at that time. The people of Bridlington would have woken up to people shouting down the streets "ship in distress," and it was calls like these that would have alerted the men who manned the lifeboat. With all of them having day jobs like carpenter, fisherman, or appren- tice, they would have most likely have been up early to start with. As soon as the news spread through the town – as in all small towns news travels fast – they would have been immedi- ately begun to get their kit together in case one of the two lifeboats needed to be launched. The sight that greeted them that morning spoke volumes. Hundreds of people began to line up along the coast, along the cliffs and beaches, watching the drama unfold. The number of people willing to lend a hand was unreal: people offered their homes to the sailors when they were brought ashore, others volunteered to go out in the boat to attempt a rescue, helping the boats' party rig equipment, and standing by in case the drama came closer to them.

Ship after ship was fighting a losing battle against the wrath of the merciless sea. Debris was already starting to wash ashore on the town's beaches, swept off the decks, or thrown by the crew to make their vessels lighter. Action had to be taken, and fast, so the lifeboatmen readied the boat and ended up having more than enough volunteers. Normally in a usual rescue, the extra men would be turned away once there was enough manpower for the crew and for the launch. But this situation was different. They were going to need all the help they could get. Young boys would volunteer, but put to one side in case they may just be needed as a last resort. They could also be used to run errands and relay messages to wives and others involved in the rescue. Everyone it seemed wanted, and could, help in some way or other, whether big or small.

The lifeboat crew were mustered and ready, and by 9am the *Robert Whitworth* had taken to the water to rescue the doomed crews, led by coxswain James Stephenson with his second cox William Miles. They headed to the priority ship, one that had already come aground, and this would be hard, harder than any other job they had been asked to do. This would test their strength to the maximum, both physically and mentally. Pulling together, the men rowed as fast and as comfortably as they could. Despite feeling they were getting nowhere fast, they persevered until at last they were almost at their target. It was the *Friends Increase*, a timber-laden sloop, bound from London to Newcastle. She had tried to head for harbour but ended up being beached near the esplanade. Coastguard rockets were unable to reach the ship so it was up to the lifeboat. Amazingly all four crew were taken off by the *Robert Whitworth* (some of the cargo was later saved too). One down, dozens to go.

As the team headed for the shore, knowing the first rescue was probably going to be the easiest one of them all, the cold was already beginning to take its toll. By this time, most people would have realised that they couldn't go on and needed a rest before continuing. But these lads never gave up, they kept on rowing, knowing that a great many lives depended on them putting every ounce of effort in possible. So they headed to their second ship. This was the *Echo*, bound from Sunderland to Rochester with coal and six crew on board. Fighting the urge to turn back in the ever-increasing storm, the wind biting at their faces, freezing their already soaking wet hands, they managed to get all the crew off in one go before once again turning to shore.

Now on the verge of exhaustion, they incredibly put to sea for a third time to rescue the crew of the *Windsor*, bound from Shields to London with coal. Once again they took all six crew off and headed for shore, to leave the ship to the mercy of the sea.

However, with three crews taken off, and many more still out there, it would be impossible to expect the men to carry on. Volunteers were gathered to replace them when the lifeboat returned. When they did make it to shore, the crew were exhausted to the point that some of them actually had to be lifted out of the lifeboat and carried away. There was no way they would return now, they had pushed themselves to the limit and fought a huge battle against nature, and managed to save 16 lives from three ships.

So far, not one life had been lost, but the day had

only just begun, for there was much more work to be done. Looking out onto the bay, the task ahead seemed impossible. Each ship was on the verge of being smashed into matchwood, each sailor clinging on for dear life to the masts, rigging, canvas, anything that was fastened down. But there was no time to debate, every second counted this day, and every life saved would be a bonus. More volunteers stepped forward to go to the rescue.

The second crew boarded the lifeboat and launched into the maelstrom, with the intention of heading for a vessel, not too far away, which was, as was most of the others, in major need of assistance. But the size and handling of the *Robert Whitworth* made the task impossible. With the vessel they were heading to now capsized, the crew could not go on. It was not just seriously putting their own lives in mortal danger, but to head out now in that boat would have been suicidal, as the wind and waves were even worse than ever. The decision was made to head back to shore and suspend any more rescues until they could launch the private lifeboat *Harbinger*.

Already worn out from trying to get to the fourth boat, the crews were taken off and the *Robert Whitworth* pulled up onto the beach. Later close by, a piece of wood bearing the name *Windsor* came ashore, a reminder of how hard they had worked and how lucky they had had it so far. They weren't about to give up now. The following men took part in the lifeboat crews:

S. Readhead	Melcha Walkington (34)
William Miles	J. Williamson
R. Scales	George A. Knowsley
J. Brown	A. Miles
R. Cammish	R. Williamson
Peter Anderson (27)	J. Usher
J. Stephenson	T. Boddy
A. Bullock	J. Ainsworth (31)
J. Wallis	J. Nicholls
Captain G. Knott	E. Hutchinson.

By this time ship after ship had been pounded by the waves, smashed up and run onto the beach, or heading towards certain death against the harbour wall, or swamped by the weight of cargo and water that had already filled their holds. Most of the boats had been run ashore by their captains in a last desperate attempt to save their crews. With the lifeboats only able to go to one ship at a time, desperate times called for desperate measures.

In a last ditch attempt to stay alive, sailors were attempting to swim for shore, clinging to wreckage, and being lost in the freezing water. In water this cold in winter, a human body's time limit is put at just minutes. The initial plunge sends the body into shock and from then on it's a downward spiral. The coastguards were ready to bring the men ashore and rockets were fired to get lines onto the ships so at least they could try save them when all other hope was lost.

But despite being so close to rescue, many more would die. The man in charge of the Rocket Lifesaving Apparatus was Chief Boatman Tyrrell, but unfor- tunately the rocket apparatus was not at its best at this point. Trying to fire them off in a storm as bad as this was almost an impossibility, and one eyewitness says they were being fired at intervals of up to 30 minutes . . . and missing each time. And these rockets were few and far between, the coastguard having just two, and they were both being used on different parts of the shore.

The *Harbinger* was finally launched at around 11am to take over the duties of the *Robert Whitworth*, which by now had been dragged back on shore. At this time hundreds more people had lined the shores, some offering help, some watching the drama unfold with horror, some watching their fathers and husbands take part in the dramatic rescues. The *Harbinger* was carried on the men's shoulders to the north beach (a journey of nearly a mile!) where she would be taken down Trinity Cut and launched from the beach.

In a backbreaking effort, the boat was sent out and the first task was rescuing a crew of five on the north side. The *Harbinger's* crew consisted normally of eight people, including fishermen William James Treamer and Christopher "Kit" Brown. Brown would later become a legend in the town for other rescues played out in the coming years.

By noon there were seven ships stranded on the

north beach and two on the south beach. It seemed that the shocking dramas were mirrored elsewhere around the coast, where towns and villages were suffering the same fate.

Four crew were saved when the schooner *Mary*, from South Shields and laden with coal, ran ashore at Filey at 1pm. Having been dismasted and out of control, she was out of reach of the rocket apparatus fired by the coastguard but the Filey lifeboat *Hollon* was dragged by six horses along the beach and launched, just in time to get to the stricken vessel. The lifeboatmen managed to get to them and rescue Captain Moore and the crew, despite the torrent of sleet and snow. The ship then sank just minutes later. At the time the gale blew up, no fewer than 32 fishing vessels were in the area. One such boat attempted to rescue the crew of a large brig. The crew were so numbed that there was no way they could launch the boat, let alone get into it and row to the fishing boat. Another such vessel, the *Mareden,* was seen heading towards Filey Brigg. Two boats went as fast as they could to attach a line and successfully towed the vessel into Scarborough harbour by the Saturday morning. The salvors then claimed £250 for their work and the captain of the brig resisited the demand. The ship had lost both topmasts and had her mainmast damaged.

Meanwhile back in Bridlington, after the first boat's crew had been rescued, they turned their attention to the five crew of a second ship. Once again after a struggle with the elements, they brought five half-dead but grateful seamen to shore. Ten-year- old Joseph Richard Bedlington, son of one of the lifeboatmen, Richard Bedlington, ran up and down both piers to relay news of his father and the boat to the waiting crowds and relatives. It was on one of these runs he met up with his father and some other survivors and ran full speed home to tell his mother to get hot blankets and a bed ready.

No sooner had another crew been landed, than a third trip was going out. This time it was a Blyth brig, the *Spinney*, and five men and a boy were saved. Again the boat landed the crew before setting out to do a fourth rescue, which was on the south side – and the crew of the *Squirrel* were saved and brought into the harbour. Kit Brown was taken out and replaced due to exhaustion at this point.

The fifth rescue was saving the crew of the Scarborough fishing vessel *Vivid*. Lifeboatman Robert Hopper did not make that trip and stayed behind to rest. The *Vivid* attempted to enter the harbour but was unable to do so and ran aground on the south beach. Her crew were all saved by the lifeboat. Captain Vary waited till all his crew had been landed safely by the lifeboat before leaving the ship. She wasn't in a bad state and there was a thought that later she may be able to be pulled off the beach and saved.

Time and again the little boat proved its worth,

returning with crew and swapping their own crew whenever exhaustion had set in. On the seventh time, one of the oarsmen, George Knowsley, had to be relieved, and David Purdon himself took his place. Just before he entered the boat he had sent a telegraph to Count Batthyany telling him of the successes the boat was having during this difficult time.

At the time the lifeboat was out at one ship, the death throes of two others would be seen. One ship struck Bridlington's north pier at around 2pm, and with no success with the rocket apparatus, the *Robert Whitworth* tried but was unable to get to them. They had to try anything possible to survive. Witnesses say a boat was launched but this quickly sank killing the two occupants. Unfortunately before anyone could reach the other four holding on for life in the rigging, the ship turned over and sank killing them all, shortly before 5pm just 30 yards from safety. This ship was later identified as the *Produce* by her papers which had washed ashore. One man, known only as "a Negro," who leaped from the wreck, was clinging to the promenade wall, when, almost in reach of rescuers trying to find a rope, a heavy piece of timber smashed his legs and dashed his body away from the wall, sweeping him to his death.

Meanwhile, in the *Harbinger*, the sixth rescue was going ahead, which was attempting to get to a collier off Wilsthorpe, and two other ships which were grounded nearby. Hopper joined the lifeboat crew for this rescue. The five crew of one ship was immediately rescued as the lifeboat was right next to her. It is possible this was the *Bebside*, which was travelling from Blyth for Tronville and had become stranded. They were then landed on south beach and they helped relaunch the *Harbinger*, which then set out again to the other brig in distress.

At this time, people were getting concerned more than ever for the men who were going out putting their own lives at risk. Margaret Atkin begged her husband Richard not to go out again. He had already been out twice, but he decided that he would anyway. He needed to give it one more try, then he might swap with someone else and rest.

This time, at 3.30pm, with sleet and snow battering their faces, they headed towards the collier again. There was nine in the crew, all exhausted but determined, led by Coxswain John Robinson, who had been on an incredible six out of the seven rescues, David Purdon, Richard Bedlington, Robert Hopper, John Clappison, James Watson, Richard Atkin, Robert Pickering and William Cobb. They immediately got on with the task in hand, as they could tell the situation with the brig was getting worse. She was the *Delta*, and her crew had tried in vain to launch their own boat. It had turned over immediately and drowned them. One man, an old sailor (some say it was the captain himself), was still on the *Delta*, and he had taken to the rigging. As the *Harbinger* approached, they called on him to jump. Three times the lifeboat pulled up to the brig. However, the man was so scared he was virtually frozen to the spot. "Jump! For God's sake jump!" they shouted but there was little hope for him. There was no time to waste: he either had to jump or he would die from the cold, if not being drowned when the ship went over.

But things were about to take a horrifying turn for the worst. At that moment, a huge wave lifted the *Harbinger* up on its end and slammed it back down again upside down. The nine crew were all flung into the sea, and all oars were swept away. When the boat was seen bobbing around upside down on the surface, only three of the lifeboatmen came up alive – Robinson, Bedlington and Hopper. More might have been saved if they had been wearing lifejackets, but they had not been provided with them, some said due to lack of funds, others said they had them but they were unfit for use. Whatever the reason, the Gale had claimed six more victims, and the day wasn't finished yet.

With the *Harbinger* upside down, the three lifeboat crew were now in a struggle to save themselves. Robert Hopper and John Robinson got on top of the upturned hull, while Robert Pickering was nearby attempting to climb on board also but getting washed off. Hopper took off his scarf in the hope he could use

it for Pickering to grab hold of. He grabbed it just in time to have it wrenched out of his hands by the *Harbinger* turning over once more. Pickering was never seen alive again. Robinson, who had put his arms into the life lines to secure him- self on the vessel, fell into the now righted boat, and was surprised to find Richard Bedlington, who had been underneath clinging on and already in the bottom. Some reports have said that air holes permitted him to hear the conversations between the two men while it was upside down. With the three of them alive out of the nine crew, and with their oars swept away, they sat and waited to drift ashore, Hopper still clinging on to his scarf. Agonisingly slow, and at the mercy of the wind and waves, they came ashore at Wilsthorpe and given shelter by a Mr Appleby's family and local man Robert Dobson. By now the men were in shock, suffering from the extreme cold and the sight of the loss of six of their colleagues and close friends. No one saw or saved the man in the rigging on the *Delta*. He never jumped and died with his shipmates.

At around the same time, at 3.30pm on the south shore, the *Margaret* came aground and the crew, bound from Seaham to Ipswich, took to the rigging. Two hours later the ship was high and dry, her captain William Mills dead, the remaining three crew rescued by 34-year-old PC Thomas Botham, who waded out with other willing men including George Leftley, a miller, and assisted them ashore, taking them to the

Cock and Lion. The three men were given food and revived before getting a bed to rest on.

A few miles away in Flamborough, local man Leonard Mainprize and three others, Thomas Woodcock, John Duke and Cockroft Warcup, carried their local lifeboat across from South Landing to the rocks, a section known as the Old Fall, where another ship, the *Arrow*, had come aground. The boat was launched and upon arrival at the wreck, Mainprize leaped up onto the rigging to cut free a man who was caught up. The other three crew were being rescued by the rocket apparatus, but tragically the line broke and the three men were trapped on the wreck. Two of these men were lashed to the mast which then broke, drowning them both.

When the *William Maitland* came aground, Captain Newton tried to get the crew to abandon ship but they refused and chose instead to take to the rigging and await rescue. The captain jumped overboard and amazingly made it to safety. The rest of the crew however died when the mast was ripped off at around 6.30pm. This is Captain Anthony Newton's account of the sinking of the *William Maitland* :

"Proceeded with favourable weather at 2am, on the 10th, when the wind had veered to the south, and at 6am increased to a gale from SSE to ESE, the ship being then about 20 miles south of Flamborough Head. Put the ship under snug canvass and with her head to the sea until noon, when they were about nine miles south of Bridlington. At noon ESE gale thick with snow, a heavy sea struck the ship, doing great damage and making a clean sweep of the deck causing the vessel to leak. Wore towards land, keeping the pumps going. At 2pm hoisted signal of distress to a screw steamer, but the latter could not assist on account of the heavy seas. The water rapidly increased in the ship, and finding we could not keep her afloat ran her ashore for the safety of their lives about 4pm about seven miles south of Bridlington. The vessel struck heavily, the sea making a clean breach over her. Tried to persuade the crew to leave the ship, and to try to reach the shore on spars. About 4.15pm jumped overboard with a lifebuoy and succeeded in reaching the shore. The coastguard came to the wreck, but were unable to reach the ship with a rocket line. The crew took to the rigging until 6.30, when they were carried overboard with the masts and drowned. The vessel broke up, and the stores washed ashore were sold by auction. Five men drowned."

A brig came ashore near Sewerby and the crew walked ashore on the ebb tide. Another ship near Sewerby came aground and the crew took to the boats. Coastguards waded in and grabbed the sailors to safety.

At 5pm came sunset but this wasn't the end of the day for the disaster. A man was seen waving a lamp as he clung to the fore yard of a schooner. The rocket line proved unsuccessful and the man was next seen clinging to wreckage with his lamp, dead, at about 7.30pm. Various unidentified wrecks occurred time after time. One was observed to the south at about 8pm when suddenly her bright light was extinguished with no sign of any of her crew after that. At around 9pm the brig *Imod* grounded at the harbour entrance. Her deck had been stripped clean by the storm and now the crew were fighting with pumps to save the stricken ship. Her bowsprit was broken and she was leaking badly. It is said that a sloop captain's wife took over and steered their vessel to safety inside the harbour. Whether it was this one nobody knows.

At 11pm another sloop was seen ashore on the south side and all her eight or nine crew rescued. Two other ships were driven ashore at Auburn and up to nine people perished. The *Spinner*, bound from Blyth to Boulogne in ballast, grounded but did not wreck. The captain of the *Rapid* had his leg broken, but he and his five crew were saved.

The *John* was seen to go down about a mile from Bridlington, the boat belonging to the ship washing ashore with the words "John, Ramsgate, Godfrey Dane," Godfrey Dane being her previous master. The *Rebecca and Elizabeth,* bound from Hartlepool to Wisbech, became wrecked and cargo lost. *Peri* was bound Seaham to Lynn, once again a total loss.

Bridlington had had her fair share of tragedy that Friday. But towns up and down the coast were suffering just as badly. From the Tees down to Norfolk, disaster was striking the ships. One after another they were wrecked, some of the crews saved by the local boats, but a lot of them sinking with no trace of life.

At Withernsea, the schooner *Henry*, of Goole, was driven ashore in the afternoon. She had been on passage from Selby to Stokes Bay, Portsmouth. The local lifeboat was launched but only one of her crew could be saved, and that was Captain George Pearson, who had jumped overboard and had drifted to shore clinging to wreckage. A servant named Thomas Gill rushed into the sea and helped him ashore.

At Hornsea the schooner *Terminus*, based in Yarmouth, came ashore at around 5pm, almost opposite the coastguard station. The crew took to the rigging and were seen to be cheering when the lifeboat was launched. However, the lifeboat was beaten back by the seas and the moment it hit the beach, the lifeboat- men jumped out. Some of the people nearby thought it was cowardice and would have taken the boat out themselves had it not been for the lifeboatmen stopping them from using their boat. At 8pm, with the six crew still clinging to the rigging with numbing hands and by now beyond exhaustion, the foremast collapsed and the rest of the crew were thrown overboard. Conflicting reports say none survived, others say four were helped ashore. The wrecked ship was driven further on the beach and smashed. A rocket line managed to get to the ship but

March 4, 1871] THE GRAPHIC 19

THE TERRIFIC STORM OF FRIDAY.

The following appeared in our Second Edition, issued at 2 30 p.m. on Saturday last.

As stated in our first edition, it was impossible to obtain accurate and connected information respecting the serious disasters and loss of life which took place yesterday in time for our ordinary issue We, however, now publish all particulars that we have been able to collect, but beyond these the fearful sacrifice of life and loss of property which have occurred within the Bay is believed to be very great, and probably will never be known. The principal cause of the said disaster appears to have arisen from the fact that, up to an early hour, the wind had been almost due west, causing vessels from the north to hug the shore when suddenly it veered round to S.S.E., blowing a terrific gale, against which a great many were powerless to bear up, and consequently were driven on shore, or have gone down with all hands on board. At noon yesterday there were seven vessels stranded on the North Beach and two on the South Beach, and by the exertions of our men with the lifeboat the crews of five were saved by Count Batthyany's boat, and two by the Whitworth boat. The crews of the other two reached the shore in their own boats. The greatest credit is due for the almost superhuman exertions made by the Quay sailors throughout the whole of the day. About two o'clock a Brig struck very near the North Pier end, and two of the crew took to their Boat, which was almost instantly swamped, and both men lost. The others remained on the vessel and the Whitworth Lifeboat made several efforts to get to them, but the wind and surf made it impossible of accomplishment, and for two or three hours the crew was in the rigging numbed with cold and crying for help. The rocket apparatus was tried, but was also unavailing, and shortly before five o'clock the vessel turned over, and went down with all hands on board. About ten o'clock a vessel was drifted on shore at Barmston and the crew was in the rigging for several hours. The rocket apparatus from Skipsea was worked, but unsuccessfully, and the Quay Lifeboat was sent for, but of course could not be taken. The whole of the crew were consequently lost. Another vessel came on shore at Wilsthorpe, but the crews of the lifeboats were so exhausted with their severe duties that it was found impossible to obtain men, until Mr. David Purdon, a journeyman in his employ from

The caption from *The Graphic* of 4th March 1871 reads: "The late storm on the Yorkshire coast - Scene from Bridlington pier."

A NEW LIFEBOAT FOR BRIDLINGTON.— A very noble present is about to be made to the town of Bridlington, by Count Batthyany, an Austrian nobleman, at present living there. The gift consists of a lifeboat, which is now being built by Mr. Purdon of Bridlington-Quay. The boat will be composed of mahogany, and will possess the usual air-tight compartments. It will be ready for launching in a short time.

the crew may not have been familiar with how it worked and therefore didn't know what to do. Arguments broke out when the lifeboatmen refused to allow volunteers to man the boat and at least try to save the crews. Just about the whole town was out to see this dramatic incident. It wasn't long before a second ship grounded and the locals waded up to the wreck waist deep to save her crew, before a third ship grounded within a mile and half of the other two.

Further up the coast at Robin Hoods Bay, the Shields vessel *Horta*, bound for London with coals, sank off the Bay, but all her crew were saved and landed ashore. Her crew were taken to Scarborough by yawl. In Scarborough itself, roofs were damaged in the gale, and skylights in the railway station were blown in. There were however no injuries.

The *Doune Castle*, a Whitby brig, came ashore at four miles north of Scarborough and became a total wreck, with no sign of the crew.

Off Grimsby, several vessels were grounding, the *Margaret Daudy*, a schooner from Arbroath carrying potatoes, sank at Cleeness, but not before her crew were saved. The brig *Sicily* travelling from Shields to London (Captain Mitchell) and the brig *Elizabeth Harrison*, bound for Calais under Captain Kilvington, both laden with coal, were both wrecked close to each other, also at Cleeness. All nine crew from *Sicily* and seven crew from the *Elizabeth Harrison* were saved.

There were several other incidents down the coast. Another *Sicily*, this one a schooner, and the brig

ONE OF THE DISASTERS OF THE 10th FEBRUARY, 1871.

The Brig "Produce," of Whitby, which was wrecked behind the North Pier, and all hands lost.
A report of the Memorial Service held last Sunday, in connection with the Disaster, appears on page 6.

THE CREW OF THE "HARBINGER" LIFEBOAT,
On the 10th February, 1871.

Reading from left to right:—1st Row (Top).—*William Cobb, *James Watson, *John Clappison, *Robert Pickering, *David Purdon (all standing up). 2nd Row.—Richard Bedlington, Robert Hopper, *Richard Atkin, and John Robinson.
Those marked with an asterisk were drowned.

Euphemia, from Hartlepool to London, were both leaking but saved by Cleethorpes fishermen. Assistance had also been successful with the schooner *Edward*, after one of her crew had been washed overboard. The captain of the German schooner *Alpha*, laden with coal for Emden, was lost overboard too.

The Hull-based vessel *Kate* was abandoned in a sinking state in the Humber and her crew saved, and another unknown vessel was seen to sink in the same area not long afterwards.

On the Lincolnshire coast, at Saltfleet, lay the sloop *Vivid* (of Grimsby) bound from Skitlerhaven for London with tiles, the schooner *Betsy Ann* (of Maldon) bound with coal from Hartlepool to Ipswich, the Goole-based *Agabas* bound for Faversham (described as a "shoddy" state), the *Benjamin Sarah* bound from Goole to London with coal, and the *Treaty* (of Goole), from Grimsby for Antwerp with wheat. Another 11 ships were reportedly aground off Grimsby.

The Lynn-based vessel *Ketch Thought* grounded near the coastguard station outside Yarmouth at around 7pm laden with coal. None of the crew were heard of again. At around the same area, at midnight near to Yarmouth harbour, the schooner *Surprise*, based at Teignmouth and laden with pipe clay, grounded. All her crew were saved. A Dutch smack later sank on entering the harbour on the Saturday. None of her crew were lost. Several other ships were seen to be sunk.

The *Two H H* sank off Dunwich, and two other unknowns went down with all hands off Lowestoft on Saturday. Papers washing ashore at Pakefield led to the belief that the brig *Zephyr* had been lost off Norfolk with all hands. The Hartlepool-based vessel was on her way to Exeter. Another Scarborough brig, the *Oronoco*, owned by Messrs Hick & Co., was wrecked off Shields but her crew were rescued.

The brig *Jabez*, of Whitby, formerly owned by Mr White of South Shields, ran onto the rocks at the east end of the Black Middens at Tynemouth, just 20 yards from the shore, and imme- diately below the Spanish Battery. She was battered and broken, foundering around 50 yards from shore, with the waves "rocking her like a cradle" in full view of the spectators, who could do nothing to help. The crew were seen to crowd on deck in a terrified manner shouting for help. The lifeboat was unable to get close enough for fear of grounding herself. The Tynemouth Volunteer Life Brigade threw a line over but the crew were not familiar with the workings of the appliance and began hauling it in. When the ship began to break up, two crew were washed overboard and clung to wreckage, coming ashore, but two others drowned, leaving the final two on deck. It wasn't long before they too were swept away and lost. The two survivors were tended to by medical staff.

The *Henry*, of Weymouth, bound from Selby to Stokes Bay, Portsmouth, with coal, grounded at

Withernsea and thanks to the coastguard, Captain William White was rescued. The lifeboat heroically battled the raging sea to help, when the captain jumped overboard and kept himself afloat by clinging to a spar. He drifted to the shore, where a local man took care of him. He was the only survivor. He later wrote to the *Hull News* giving a personal thanks to the coastguard and Captain Banyard.

On Middleton Beach, near Hartlepool, the two ships *Stanley* and *Jane Ann* grounded after a failed attempt to enter the harbour. Both were coal laden, and each had eight crew, all of whom were rescued and brought ashore. Shortly after noon at Shields, the schooner *John Elliotson*, of Whitstable, was seen making for the harbour under sail, when the force of the wind carried her further to the north and ran her aground. The lifeboats went out to her but because she wasn't in immediate danger the crew declined help and were able to free the ship and bring her safely into harbour.

One person who thought the Great Gale was not as bad as some he'd been in was John Newby, who was riding the storm out in the fishing yawl *William Clewes*, and eventually landed at Grimsby. This man was either in a calmer area than most or he was simply a survivor who thought bigger of himself for surviving!

The schooner *Admiral Codrington* came ashore at Shields and became a total wreck. She had left the Tyne like everyone else on Thursday but when the gale struck it was decided to turn back for home and she had grounded. When a line was passed over to them, once again the crew were unfamiliar with the workings. However, when the first man came across it was the captain of the vessel, saying he had to come across because the crew did not know what they were doing! In the end all five souls on board were rescued. They later described how the sea had carried away their rudder as they were passing and drifted onto rocks. Also at Shields, the *Light and Sign* grounded on Herd Sand, but was pulled off by the steam tug *Samson* before safely entering Shields Harbour.

At around 4am, the barque *Launceston,* which had left Shields on 6th February bound for Carloforte, grounded on the Hasborough Sands at Yarmouth, and within minutes a second coal-laden barque, the *Agincourt*, ran into her. Both ships were hard aground and in the collision one of the crew of the *Agincourt* ended up on the *Launceston*. At 5am the crew of *Launceston* abandoned ship, with the exception of Captain Johnson and his steward. They stayed on board until 8am when they launched a small boat and saved themselves at last. They were picked up by a passing brig *Corunna* of Whitby. It was not known if the crew in the boat or the crew of the *Agincourt* survived at the time and it was feared they had all drowned. However, the 14 crew in the boat had rowed until being picked up at about 9.30am by the *North Hasborough Light Ship*. Also on board was James Lee, one of the ten crew of the *Arctic Hero*, also wrecked on the Sunday close by at Great Yarmouth, the other nine of her crew having been saved. The captain and steward were landed at Shields on Sunday. All the survivors had lost all their clothes, but alive and well, and all were safely landed on shore. The *Launceston* was owned by a Mr William Wright of West Dock, South Shields, and was 571 tons and the *Agincourt* was owned by a Mr Tate of North Shields.

Off Hartlepool, the West Hartlepool pilot coble *Hood* got into difficulties and her three crew were rescued just minutes before she capsized and sank.

The Lynn ketch *Thought* was found deserted off Yarmouth, although when she passed the harbour there were people seen on board. It was assumed they had taken to the boat and had all drowned. The following morning a pair of women's boots and a woman's belt were among the things found in the wreckage, leading to speculation that there may have been a female on board. What was left of the hull would be sold at auction on the Saturday. Any hope of the crew surviving were dashed when the ship's boat was washed ashore at Kessingland.

The schooner *Surprise*, bound Teignmouth to Sunderland with clay, parted from her cables and drove ashore at the north sands at Yarmouth. Her six crew managed to get off the wreck when they were taken care of. The wreck was subsequently stripped and sold at auction on 15th February to a Mr Bonney of Gorleston. The surf lifeboat *Duff* had been to the

Thought and was seen to be not needed and then turned to the *Surprise*, again not needed.

The brig *British Queen*, bound Sunderland for London with coal, was putting in early Friday morning and reached the Tyne bar approx 1pm. In crossing the bar a light ship from the north came in the way and in endeavouring to avoid a collision, *British Queen* was driven into the Prior's Haven, where she grounded. All her crew were rescued but the captain had one of his legs crushed between the lifeboat and the ship while trying to rescue his son-in-law, who was one of the crew.

Meanwhile back in Bridlington, the gale began to die down overnight. The survivors of the shipwrecks were accommodated by the local inns and were then sent on to their homes by Mr Postill, agent of the Shipwrecked Mariners Society. The biggest disaster ever to strike the town in living memory had devastated its close-knit local community. Six local men, heroes to all who knew them, were gone. It would be up to the sea to give them up now, or keep them for eternity.

In all the dramatic events that day, the only record of the disaster in the harbourmaster's log is as follows:

"Frid 10 – A light breeze from the Eastward and cloudy, at 2am ESE, fresh, at 8am blowing a heavy gale with snow and sleet, and a heavy sea, a many ships came on shore, life boat saved a many hand but a many were drowned, lifeboat upset and six were drowned out of her, latter part more moderate."

Chapter 3

Aftermath

On the Saturday morning the beaches up and down the

Yorkshire coast were littered with wreckage, most of all at Bridlington, which had suffered the worst of it. The storm had gone, the weather calmed and the skies cleared to reveal the full enormity of the disaster. When the tide receded, hundreds of tons of coal littered the beaches. The sand in some places would remain black for years to come with the quantity of coal. Because of this, locals were allowed to take away as much as they liked. Among the wreckage on the beach a piece of wood was found carved with the words "swear not at all." A wheel cover bearing the words *Harmonia* of Hamburg was found, but it was thought to have been lost off a passing ship and not a wreck. The cover of a capstan was picked up with the words "*Hammonia*, Hamburg" and two flags painted on it. Part of a boat's stern came ashore at Whitby marked "*Horta*, South Shields." At Filey, the wrecked *Mary* was dismantled after her decks had been washed off and stern knocked out. The *Urania*, grounded at Bridlington, had her cargo saved, then was towed into the harbour on 18th February and sold as a wreck. The *Spinner* also managed to be taken off the beach and into the harbour. Upon inspection, it was found that this ship had very little damage. Another vessel, the brig *Spinney*, in ballast, was high up on the south beach, masts still standing, the most intact of all the groundings. At 9am on Saturday morning the brig *Imod* was brought into harbour in a very disabled state

The Whitby brig *Doune Castle* had successfully ridden out the storm but when bad weather returned on Sunday, 12th February, she sank after battling leaks. All her five crew were rescued by the schooner *Tweed*, which landed them in Hartlepool on Sunday night. On 30th March, a local business- man Mr William Taylor held an auction of items salved from the wrecks. Anchors and chains from the *Delta*, and several other items from various ships such as pumps, kedges, chains, anchors, rigging, canvas etc.

It was now the more horrific task that sat upon the towns-people of Bridlington: the recovery and identification of the bodies which had started to come ashore. In twos and threes they washed ashore, bloated, battered and bruised. They were laid out in the back of The Albion public house on Hilderthorpe Road, and, in the days that followed, relatives of the victims would come and identify their loved ones. The clothes of the deceased were hung on rails, still wet, tattered and merely rags. The list of clothes reads as follows: 1, Clothes of engineer, marked SE supposed to have belonged to one of the crew of a steamer which is said to have been lost with the others. His blue jacket had brass buttons upon it representing a Chinese scene. 2, Drawers and shirt marked WNH. 3, Drawers marked SB. 4, Blue flannel shirt marked DI. 5, Blue striped shirt marked WR. 6, Blue striped shirt marked WC. 7, Flannel shirt and stockings marked WL. 8, Pair of stockings marked AG.

Of the 25 bodies found on the Saturday, three were captains, and another was David Purdon.

A Mrs Fisher, "from the north," arrived on Tuesday morning to identify two of her sons, aged 17 and 19. (Was this Mrs Coleman, who had two boys on the *John*?)

All the bodies lay in their coffins, and for identification purposes they were photographed, four together, on the Monday night by local photographer John Waite Shores, of 2 Marlborough Terrace, Bridlington. Further photographs were taken on Tuesday. He would also photograph the funeral procession and provide an accurate visual account of the disaster's aftermath.

The disaster was brought home even more so when the bodies of the lifeboatmen were washed ashore.

On Sunday 12th, snow was laying thickly. James Watson's body was found, with at least four others. Two of them were thought to belong to a fishing smack which sank at North Pier. Another appeared to be around 16, well dressed, wearing Wellington boots, thought to have been a passenger. Also found that day were papers belonging to the *Teresita*, which had previously been an unidentified wreck. Relatives of John Clappison arrived during the week from Sigglesthorne to put every effort into finding his body. Rewards were offered for the finding of Clappison and William Cobb, who would not be found until several weeks after the disaster.

Thomas Thompson of the *Lavinia* was identified by a medal in his pocket from the Shipwrecked Fishermen and Mariners Royal Benevolent Society. His son, William, travelled from Seaham to formally identify him. But many of the victims would never be identified, and even today the people on these ships have no name.

On 20th February, the bodies of three men were found washed ashore in the morning. The stockings on the guernsey of one were marked JM, another had a horseshoe pattern scarf pin, and in his pocket a leather tobacco pouch, a German silver pen- cil holder, and a small brooch in his purse. The third body had nothing to identify him.

That Saturday, the first inquest was held before Mr Jennings. Robert Hopper, one of the *Harbinger* survivors, said at the inquest: "All went right, and we rescued the crew from a brig which had gone ashore while we were proceeding to the other. After landing that crew we put off again and succeeded in reaching the other vessel. There was only one man on board, the rest having been lost in their own boat. We succeeded in getting a rope from the vessel and told the man to jump into the lifeboat. But he was either unable or afraid and did not jump, and the next moment a great sea broke over us, turning the lifeboat over, and throwing the men out of her. I succeeded in getting hold of the upturned boat, and held out my scarf to John Robinson, and helped him to reach the boat and take hold. The boat was three or four minutes bottom upwards and when it righted we found Richard Bedlington inside, where he had been all the time."

This was the first of many inquests to be held in Bridlington in the coming months as more and more victims washed ashore. The next task was the funerals.

The first one to be buried was David Purdon, on 13th February; he was buried in the Priory Church grounds. The mass funeral of the gale victims took place the day after, on Tuesday, 14th February 1871. A dull and cloudy day, all shops closed for three hours as the majority of the tradesmen followed the bodies to the graves. Twenty-three of the dead were interred in the Priory grounds. Between three and four thousand people attended.

The cortege left the Albion at two o'clock led by the Chief Lord of the Manor Mr George Robinson, Lloyds agent Mr. Brambles, Dr Nelson, Messrs. Frost, Porrett and the tradesmen of Bridlington and the Quay, Committee of the Sailors' and Working Men's

Club, members of the club, members of the Amicable Society, the corpse of James Watson (which left Regents Terrace, meeting the main procession on the top of King Street), relatives and friends, and the coffins of three captains followed by 19 sailors on wagons. Behind them were relatives, friends, seamen and others. People lined the streets all the way up to Priory Church. Captain Howard of the *Margaret* belonged to the Ancient Order or Foresters and so that body paid the last respect to their brother by following him to the grave.

The procession went down Prospect Street, up towards the Priory and under the Bayle before arriving at the church. The vicar, Rev. Frederick H. Barnes, conducted the service. Watson, Captain Wm Flisher (*Produce)*, Wm Mills, Captain Wm Howard (*Margaret*), Captain Anthony Hindson (*Lavinia*), Captain Wm Calvert (*Delta*), Thomas Thompson, Richard Lindup, Simon Butterwick, Martin Burke, Michael Gerald, William Sash, and seven unknown sailors were then laid to rest in the Priory grounds. All the strangers were interred in a piece of ground purchased by Captain R. N. Beauvais of Bridlington, and presented to the town. This ground was lying close to the churchyard, and taken into it, for the purpose of burying sailors "not belonging to this place." During the service, when the coffins of the 19 unknown seamen who were buried in one grave at the east end of the church yard were all lowered, the sextons immediately began filling in the earth. This was considered harsh as the service had not yet ended, and one man stepped forward kindly requesting them

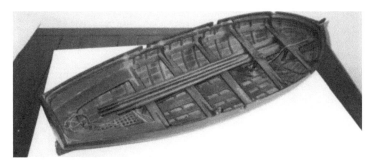

The *Harbinger* model held by the Lords Feoffees.

Display board in Pembroke Gardens.

The *Harbinger* on davits on the harbour wall.

The *Seagull* before and after the 1898 disaster.

Bedlington's mother

Richard Bedlington (left)
and Robert Hopper

Richard Bedlington's son
Joseph, who was 12 at the time
of the Great Gale

Leonard Mainprize with his son.

This is the most well known image of the Great Gale of 1871. This postcard uses an image by J.T. Allerston.

to stop, which they did until the service was over. (When the grave was being made for the 19 men, a large quantity of bones was found, it being in a part of the church yard which had once belonged to it, afterwards had been built upon and now back to its former use.)

The bodies of the three captains were buried together, Watson opposite the north porch of the church, and Purdon at the west end of the yard. These funerals would go on until May when more victims would wash ashore. Inquests would be conducted, most just ending with a "drowned 10th February" verdict. Most of them would be interred as unknown victims. Atkin was buried on 16th, James Maldon (*Caroline*) and two unknowns on 21st, Robert Pickering on 24th, unknown sailors buried 9th, 14th, 26th March and 7th April, Thomas Jameson (*Delta*) and an unknown on 13th, another unknown on 16th, William Cobb on 17th, unknown on 19th, Robert Court (*Produce*) and three unknowns on 20th, another unknown on 21st April and an unknown boy of around 17 years old found a month later and buried on 26th May.

In the meantime, funds were set up to help the families of the lifeboat crew, some collecting house to house. The market alone netted £50. Richard Atkin's widow, Margaret, received £202 and 19 shillings from the widows and orphans fund, two children received £33 16s 6d each and the other three £67 13s 0d each.

However, the debate on the future of the town's lifeboats raged on, and on 15th February a large number of the sailors and fishermen in Bridlington Quay attended at the Sailors and Working Mens Club rooms, to organise a plan whereby the *Harbinger* might be rendered more efficient. The meeting was attended by lifeboat coxswains, Rev Yarburgh Gamaliel Lloyd Graeme, and RNLI inspector Captain John Ross Ward. Mr W. Woodcock, president of the club, presided, and Mr J. W. Postill, the secretary, gave a brief statement on the history of the boat. Although plans were in the air to render the vessel seaworthy again, another new lifeboat had been promised by the Rev. Lloyd-Graeme and three different models of the proposed boat were in the room for inspection. A vote of thanks was given to John Robinson for his hard work in the keeping of the boat over the last two years. It was noted about the lack of oars and life- jackets in the boats. The crew of the national lifeboat supported a new self-righting boat as opposed to the suggested surf boat design. Ward put the idea forward of the institution managing both boats but this was decided against. Ward was understood to say that it was the custom of the Institution to send an inspector to any place where loss of life had occurred through the unsuccessful workings of their lifeboat. The coxswain, J. Stephenson, was asked how the *Robert Whitworth* had acted on the day of the storm, and he replied that she had acted well until the last trip, when the wind was so high and a strong flood tide with heavy sea that she could not get off. Many of the crews did mention that the *Whitworth* was sometimes difficult to handle and at one point came back to shore broadside on; another time the boat had to be turned completely round to go back to shore. There was a further meeting on 22nd February, to which Count Batthyany wrote a letter saying if the *Harbinger* would be placed into the hands of the club he would pay for a carriage so her efficiency would be increased. From that day the *Harbinger* lay in Bridlington harbour as a work boat.

In the meantime another tragic part to the story emerges. While the men were debating the lifeboats and better ways to save lives at sea, the widows of the dead lifeboatmen were picking up the pieces. Now they had to fend for themselves, the only men in the house being the sons, some not even old enough to work. But it was the widows of David Purdon and James Watson who would carry an even more tragic toll. Harriet Purdon died during the birth of their fourth child eight weeks after the gale. She was buried with David on 12th April, aged 29. However, the Priory burial register reads "died of grief two months after her husband was drowned in the Great Gale." Their two children Annie and Frederick were brought up by their Aunt Charlotte and her husband Josephus Scholefield.

James Watson's wife Eliza became mentally ill after the love of her life had died at the hands of the gale, and she was admitted at the request of her brother Thomas to the North Riding Lunatic Asylum at Clifton, York, on 21st February. Described as a

Wesleyan Methodist, this was her first attack of mental illness, and had been suffering for around six days, having not previously been under treatment. Eliza was admitted as a private patient No 1370, with the supposed cause being the sudden loss of her husband in the *Harbinger*, and although not suicidal, she was considered a danger to others. The following are the details of medical records and reports for Eliza Watson: Two medical certificates form part of the reception order. The first was by George Dawson Nelson, MRCS Eng (Member of the Royal College of Surgeons) and LSA Lond. (Licentiate of the Society of Apothecaries), in practice as a surgeon (GP). He examined Eliza, and certified her as a lunatic on the following grounds: the facts observed by him were she had extreme violence of manner and gesticulation with indications of danger to those around. She had incoherence of language accompanied by vague assertions and ideas expressed with complete change of moral principles. The facts communicated to him by others were "continued restlessness and the fact that her maternal parent has been the subject of insanity." This was communicated to him by Thomas H. Willis and Mrs Thomas Boddy.

The other medical certificate was by John Allison, Licentiate of the Faculty of Physicians and Surgeons of Glasgow, who examined her the same day (21st February). He observed that her language was incoherent, her replies to questions were unintelligible and her gesticulations violent and threatening. Thomas

H. Willis had communicated to him that she passed her time in singing, praying, and using bad language and violently refused food when offered to her.

The reception order contains replies to a series of printed questions. She had no children. She could read and write. Her mother had been similarly afflicted. There were no previous symptoms before the attack such as depression, alteration in temper or feelings etc. In answer to a question about symptoms it says "symptoms given." In answer to a question about raving on particular or general subjects, it says on general subjects. She was not prone to tearing clothes, breaking furniture etc. She was "clean," i.e. attentive to the calls of nature. She had made no attempts at self destruction or made any threats of injury. She had refused food "always." Her bodily health was "tolerably good." Her natural temper was "kind, gentle and humane." She had followed her occupation up to the present. She had no oddity or eccentricity before. She had no periodical attacks of any other disease. The illness was not due to childbed or injury to the head. The medical remedies used so far had been cold lotions, with no apparent benefit.

It was then noted that she had been suffering from an attack of acute mania. She was in a very feeble state of bodily health due to her refusal of sufficient food, continued raving and sleep- lessness. She raved about all sorts of subjects about her husband, religion etc. Her conversation was noisy and totally incoherent. Her skin was hot, her face flushed, pulse 100, weak, refused feeding. She had brandy, beef tea and arrowroot. She was also being given chloral hydrate to sedate her.

On 22nd February, it was noted that the chloral draught procured some sleep the previous night; she required feeding but would take it from the spoon. The next day she was less excited and took food without much resistance. On 24th February she was not so well, and refusing and wasting food when fed with a spoon. She was fed that afternoon with a pump, with about one quart of a mixture of beef tea and arrowroot with brandy.

On 25th February she had a better night and was fed again; on 26th she was much better, more rational and took her food without feeding. On 27th she was very weak having been noisy and restless all night; she took tea and beef tea in the night but wasted nearly all that given to her in the morning. She was fed with the stomach pump with two pints of beef tea, arrowroot and 3oz brandy. On 28th she had a bad night and was much exhausted; too weak to be fed with the pump and almost unable to swallow anything. She was to have brandy and water every quarter of an hour. Her pulse was almost imperceptible; she was totally unconscious and her respiration laboured. She was soon after seized with a convulsion which lasted up to a minute and when it passed she rallied and her pulse became better, though weak, and consciousness returned and she became loquacious and raved as before. Brandy and egg was constantly given to her, but she again became unconscious, rallied and remained in that state until the evening when she rather suddenly died.

Twenty hours after her death a post mortem was carried out and her cause of death was given as 1) acute mania; 2) arachnitis (referring to convulsions?); and 3) exhaustion. This was signed by Medical Superintendent H. Clifford Gill.

Once again the Great Gale had claimed yet another victim. The papers reported her death and said she left "no family." She was buried with her late husband, her grave stating her date of death to be 1st March.

Bridlington harbour in the 19th Century.

Prince Street leading down to the harbour in the 19th Century..

Capsizing of the *Harbinger* during the *Delta* rescue.
Painting by J. T. Allerston.

Gale painting by J. T. Allerston. The ship could be the *Produce*.

Two Gale paintings by Bridlington artist John Cooper.

Two Gale paintings by Bridlington artist John Cooper.

The Albion today. Bodies were brought here after the disaster.

Bathyanny Villa in Scarborough today.

Bridlington lifeboat station today.

The old coastguard station at the time of the Gale is now a café (note the anchor on the wall).

Trinity Cut today. The bridge was built in 1888

Bridlington Bay today from the same location as the scene on pages 58-59. Note the remains of the railing in the ground.

North Street at the site of Purdon's yard, now a branch of Iceland.

Various references to the Great Gale are still found today,
including this painting in the Harbour Heritage Museum and
the tapestry in Bridlington Priory.

Chapter 4

Legacy

Each year on the Sunday closest to 10th February, a memorial service is held at Priory Church for the victims of the gale. This event is usually attended by volunteers from the present Bridlington lifeboat, who give a brief run down of that year's successes, and the town's mayor. Prayers are said, hymns are sung and then the procession is led outside for a minute's silence and a few words at the Great Gale memorial, a stone obelisk giving the names of the lifeboatmen who died and listing some of the known ships to come to grief. This was paid for by public subscription and stands above the graves of the drowned men. Nearby in the churchyard are five graves of the *Harbinger* crew. Although the men are not buried together, some stones were moved so they are all next to each other. This day has also become known by some as "Fishermen's Sunday." This memorial service was revived in 1981 after it not being observed for some years.

Bridlington would have the *Robert Whitworth* replaced by the *John Abbot*, which stayed in Bridlington from August 1871 to 1885. The *Harbinger* would be replaced by the *Seagull*, paid for by the Rev. Lloyd-Graeme.

Today the pathway on the south side of the seafront beyond the Spa Hall bears testimony to one man's bravery and is dedicated to Kit Brown. In December 1893, Kit Brown, Fred Brown, Richard Purvis, Tom Clark and John Usher would get the silver medal of the RNLI for rescuing the six crew from the stranded schooner *Victoria*. Tragically, Kit Brown was killed during a storm on 25th March 1898 while attempting to rescue the crew of the *Seagull* lifeboat. The *Seagull* became the last lifeboat to be privately owned in Bridlington, and the town wouldn't get two lifeboats again for around a century. However, the story of the Great Gale lives on in various parts of the small town. The walls of the RNLI boat house are decorated with every rescue undertaken and the number of lives saved. One section reads :

1871 Feb 10th	Barge............	"Friends Increase"	London
" " "	Brigantine ..	"Echo"	Maldon
" " "	Brig............	"Windsor"	Lynn

Today the Bridlington lifeboat is based on Marine Drive on the south shore and consists of two boats, an offshore vessel and an inshore vessel. The RNLI continues to save lives at sea to this day, but better technology and working with the Humber coastguard and emergency services means that fewer lives are lost than ever before.

The figurehead from the wreck of the *Margaret* is today on display in the Bayle Museum along with another head from the *Delta*. David Purdon's model of the *Harbinger* is kept at the head office of the Lords Feoffees. The knife which Leonard Mainprize used in the rescue of the crewman of the *Arrow* was given to Tom Woodhouse, a local fish mer- chant and lifeboat secretary, who donated it to the Sewerby Hall Museum where it remains on display today. Leonard Mainprize himself would later die with his son Leonard Jnr, 24, in a coble together on 28th August 1903.

Figure- heads from *Margaret* and *Delta*.

The Harbinger Arms is a public house attached to the Revelstoke Hotel opposite Trinity Church. The board outside once portrayed the lifeboat going to the rescue of the *Delta*.

The Bridlington Har- bour Museum has a Great Gale display sporting a figurehead of a lion clutching a shield of St George, from one of the wrecks, the knife handle found by th4e author, and other photographs depict- ing disaster. This small build- ing offers a good insight into the history of the harbour and surrounding area and boasts a few artefacts from several of the wrecks from the First World War including the pro- pellor from the U-boat *UC-39*.

A figure head from the *Produce* was placed in or near the home of a Captain Birkenhead at Hilderthorpe. Unfortunately this has never been seen since and it is thought to have been thrown out over

Figurehead from an unknown gale wreck in the Harbour Museum.

The Harbinger Arms at the Revelstoke Hotel.

the years. The old newspaper found in Marton Grange Hotel now hangs in a frame on the wall with a full copy next to it to compare the two.

The knife found by the author in 2006.

Great Gale display at the Harbour Heritage Museum.

Bridlington painter John Taylor Allerston drew scenes from photographs he had taken of the gale, and these paintings are today considered a true representation of what the scene was like that day. These paintings are now in possession of the Feoffees. He died in 1914 aged 86. He is thought to have painted around 2400 pictures. They always seem to draw a crowd when places like the local tourist attraction Sewerby Hall have them on dis- play!

The *Robert Whitworth* was taken to Carnsore, County Wexford, and renamed *Iris*, in 1874. She remained at this station until 1890 and saved over 70 people in various rescues, including the Tuskar Rock Lighthouse. The station itself closed in 1897 after 38 years.

After the gale, the *Harbinger* lay on the side of the harbour and was later rested on the Raft Yard, Rope Walk. On 28th October 1888, a Club committee meeting said that the boat should no longer be used as a lifeboat as the vessel had now been examined and decided it was not suitable to do the job. They would inform the Count and express thanks for the boat and the service it had provided.

Mr Leonard Taylor then bought her and moved her to a yard on St Johns Avenue (later the venue of the ladies' "25 club" around 1902. Mr Jack Nettleton, No 8 The Bungalows, took it by road to Malton for service with a farmer, but it was too heavy to be used as a raft on that part of the river. She was then taken to Stamford Bridge to be used as a house boat. Later it was sent up river to Kirkham Priory for the same purpose. It was swept away in floods and sank with a second boat, which was never recovered. The old lifeboat was unfit for any use and came into possession of Charles Lazenby, who started to break it up for firewood, having no idea of the history of the boat.

The *Harbinger* itself was found in January 1935 by a Mr Alfred Hudson of Bridlington at Kirkham Abbey. In a press interview, Mr Lazenby said: "the vessel has carved on the side the figures '26.4 x 6, 10 x 3.9 29 persons.' I know that the vessel originally came from Bridlington, but I do not know what it was or what it was called. I think it came from Stamford Bridge about 30 years ago and then disappeared in the floods. It has been a strong sea boat, made of spruce, and has a square back." The gunwhale and rudder were exhibited on the 64th anniversary at the Spa Royal Hall. It was brought to Bridlington by local RNLI secretary C. H. Gray, the captain of the Rocket Lifesaving Company F. J. Wilkinson, and two other men, G. Anderson and

Linford. It was proved beyond shadow of a doubt when it was examined that the wood was mahogany and the original brass plates were still attached. On one piece of wood were the words "29 passengers." However, people did doubt whether this was the *Harbinger*, but it turned out that the boat had a square stern because upon her new role as a house boat, her air box on the stern was sawn off to give a square hull shape. However, that is where the trail goes cold and the remains of the boat haven't been seen since. Should the pieces still exist, they would take pride of place in the town's museums.

As for the heroes of the Great Gale, PC Botham would get a bronze medal from the Royal Humane Society for his actions in saving the crew of the *Margaret*.

George Leftly would get a certificate awarded to him at the Alexandra Hotel in July 1871.

Captain John Robinson died on 15th February 1890 (death certificate says 25th). He became increasingly frail and weak and suffered a stroke(?). He was 76 and living at 1 Alma Terrace. He is buried in the grounds of Bridlington Priory, but his grave is not marked or recorded exactly. His death

certificate gives the cause of death as "paralysis."

Robert Hopper, who went on to become cox of the Barmston lifeboat for eight years, died on 20th August 1898 at home. His death certificate records "Haemorrhoids 3 years, cardiac asthe- nia." He was 63, living at 9 Ferndale Terrace. He was buried in Bridlington cemetery, and his funeral was attended by Richard Bedlington, at the time the last survivor of the *Harbinger*. Bedlington would himself pass away on 26th July 1900 (death certificate says 24th) at his home at 5 Pembroke Terrace. His death certificate says cause of death was "senile decay and heart disease." He was 78.

Rev Lloyd-Graeme would die on 30th May 1890 at the age of 76 after a lifetime of serving his local town, both spiritually and financially. A window in the Priory bears his name, and is himself buried at the church in his home village of Sewerby. A well-respected man, he would be sadly missed for years to come. Count Batthyany, the man who saved so many lives by donating funds, died on 27th August 1906, also of senile decay.

David Purdon's business on North Street was turned over to John Brown, who worked in a similar trade, and Harriet said she had every confidence in recommending him as her late husband's successor as from 27th February 1871. Purdon's Yard and the Central Methodist Church, closed in 1970 and demolished, on the corner of North Street/Chapel Street, is now the supermarket Iceland. Purdon's daughter Annie died on 31th May 1925. The last lifeboatman from that fateful day was George Knowsley, who lived until aged 89 when he passed away on 29th July 1926.

So the last people to remember the Great Gale from memory have come and gone. We can only imagine what the scenes were like, what people had to go through for a small town to cope with such an immense tragedy. We see today such towns such as Dunblane, Lockerbie, Aberfan, and see how they coped with disaster, and realise that Bridlington is not so different after all. It was all down to heroism why the death toll wasn't much higher. But on the other hand, it was all down to greedy ship owners why ships had just about fallen to pieces in a rotten state in the first place. But the memory does live on with us today, and the discovery of small news articles from years gone by tell us that events such as this will never just be swept under the carpet.

On 9th February 1936 a grand concert was held in commemoration of the 75th anniversary at the Spa Royal Hall, organised by the Bridlington Rocket Life Saving Company, and the RNLI. This was repeated the year after on 7th February, and in 1938 on 13th February, again in 1939. Then in March of 1995 came the Bridlington Town Play, named *Come Hell or High Water*. This told the story of the lifeboat through the Great Gale and up to the death of Kit Brown. The play ran for 11 nights and was seen by over 3,000 people. Mike Wilson played his hero Kit Brown, an event he says which changed his life for ever. And in June 2003 a Radio 4 programme told the story of Count Batthyany and the *Harbinger* lifeboat.

But perhaps the major legacy, which the Gale contributed to immensely, was that the disaster itself showed Derby MP Samuel Plimsoll that unless something was done, and quickly, thousands more sailors would die in their so-called "coffin ships." He fought tooth and nail for a load line to be painted on any and all ships plying the trade routes. The more he was ignored, the harder he tried. He became known as the sailors', and admitted that he couldn't sleep at night knowing there were most likely ships in distress and no one doing anything about it. But after putting enormous pressure on the government, his campaign was successful. A fixed load line was made law and today that line, now known as the Plimsoll Line, is standard design on all ships no matter how big or small. It is ironic that Bridlington's disaster should be part of a world-wide safety feature on all ships. Never again would greedy profit- making owners force reluctant crews to sea for the sake of an extra few pounds. And never again would so many ships be wrecked under the noses of decent people.

Over the years ship safety is getting better and better. Many of the ships wrecked that day had crews who were unfamiliar with the workings of the rocket apparatus, and some were even strangers to swimming. It is the ignorance of these essential skills that has cost so many people their lives. Sadly it would take many more disasters at sea to make stricter safety measures more adherent.

The sinking of the *Titanic* in 1912 proved to the world that no ship was safe from the elements. Not enough lifeboats and the belief that the ship was just too big to be sunk were the main factors in the huge loss of life. Thanks to regulations brought in after that, there are now more than enough lifeboats and life- jackets for everyone on board ships, as well as a 24-hour manned radio on all ships. The international ice patrol was also set up. It is just a shame it takes a tragedy before action is taken. Surely somebody somewhere could predict what would happen if ships go to sea overloaded, with an untrained crew into the path of a storm and leave them in a bay at anchor with no way out. Unfortunately not. But thankfully the lessons of history are being learned. Ships still sink, but you very rarely hear of a loss of life due to bad safety features. Maybe people do sit up and listen after all.

Today Bridlington lifeboat crews conduct regular exercises and maintain the lifeboats to the best of their abilities. The RNLI now works closely with the Maritime Coastguard Agency, Royal Air Force and Royal Navy. With communications and safety better than they have ever been, deaths at sea today are counted in ones and twos around Britain. Not in dozens per town.

From the memoirs of Fred Brown, son of Kit Brown

And now for a gale in Bridlington Bay. Never before or after was there so much wreckage on the beach; never before or after has there been so many lives lost in one day; and never before or never after has there been so many noble ships lost with all their crews.

Let me try and give you some idea of that day, 10th February 1871. Many ships lay at the mouth of the Tyne waiting for a fine fare wind, many loaded with coal for France, London and southern ports. The morning of 9th February broke fine and clear with a fine north-west wind. The ships got their anchors and made sail, all the captains looking for a fine sharp run to their places of destination. They sped down the coast at a spanking pace and they made a fine sight in the morning sun with all sails set. But I am very sorry to say many of these ships never reached their ports.

By 10th February 1871 they had reached Bridlington Bay, known all around the coast as the Bay of Safety. But the winds died and they were all becalmed with sails hanging idly down. Then, when the wind did come, it could not have come from a worse quarter. It came in from the east and soon it was blowing a gale. The masters of these ships knew they were in a death trap, for they knew these ships could not get off a lee shore. Then the snow and hail started to come down, making things worse, and the crews also knew that they were facing death.

The lifeboat was called out to one stricken vessel and saved the crew of six. They had hardly got the rescued crew ashore when another ship was seen through the driving hail. Again the lifeboat went on its errand of mercy through the heavy seas, again bringing to shore another crew they had saved from death. Again through the rain and sleet, another ship was seen making for the harbour but, the tide being half ebb, she struck the bottom. Again the lifeboat was called out to her help and rescued five of her crew. Then the lifeboat was taken out of the water and her exhausted crew were taken home to get some food and dry clothes.

There was also another small lifeboat called the *Harbinger. M*ore ships were coming in in distress. The captains of these ships knew that their only chance of rescue was to run these ships aground. One of the ships tried to beach on the south shore, a fatal mistake that lost the lives of her crew. The lifeboat was launched about eleven in the morning and soon had rescued the crews of three vessels. She was taken out to wrecked vessels time and time again. My father went three times one after another, when the secretary told him to go home and get dry clothes on as there were plenty of willing volunteers. Hardly pausing for a rest, the crews took her out time and time again and as one oarsman became exhausted another took his place.

Still the gale grew stronger and each wreck became more difficult to get alongside: a brig, a schooner called the *Echo,* and the *Squirrel*, a fishing smack, and another collier. The lifeboat was going again when she was lifted on the crest of a wave. She was hidden from sight. One ship's crew thought the lifeboat could not see them so they took to their own boat and they washed ashore on the south beach.

The lifeboat was rushing again over the seas to a ship in distress but could not get along side for the heavy seas so the coxswain told the crew to jump and they were safely landed. Another ship's crew took to their own little boat, which turned over and all were drowned. But one old man kept to the ship's rigging and the lifeboat's crew threw a rope and dragged him through the seas, and he was saved.

On another trip, the lifeboat went to a brig called the *Delta*. When close to the ship, a monstrous wave lifted the lifeboat up in the air. As she came close to the doomed ship, another large wave brought her down again. Spectators on the shore held their breath and suddenly with a sickening crash a large wave broke over the lifeboat and in a moment she overturned. Six of her crew were washed away and were lost. One man clung to her keel and held another by his belt and they drifted away from the wreck. Another mighty wave hit the lifeboat and turned her up again on an even keel. Another of her crew was inside her. These men were the only survivors of the terrible disaster. When the boat was washed ashore she was too badly damaged to be of any further use. My father would have been in her again but, as I told you earlier, he had gone home to get dry clothes and a hot drink.

Still the ships came crashing to the beach. One struck near the sea wall and they got a rocket line over her, but before they could get the breeches buoy to her, the ship broke up, throwing her crew into the sea before the anguished townsfolk. Darkness came down.

In the morning, the beach was strewn with more wood and coal than was ever seen before. The fishermen and their wives searched among the wreckage for the bodies of the lifeboat crew and others, but many poor men were never found. Later a mass funeral was held in our Priory Church, with nearly all the townspeople attending. All the bodies were buried in a common grave and ever since that day on the Sunday that falls nearest to 10th February there has been a service of remembrance.

The total number of lives lost was never known. Over twenty vessels were lost in Bridlington Bay and between forty and fifty sailors were buried with the lifeboat crew. Over one hundred vessels were lost on that day along the coast, but nowhere was as bad as Bridlington Bay.

My mother told me that she and five other fishermen's wives helped to wash and lay out the bodies of most of the poor sailors for burial. They had perished in the worst disaster that had ever befallen the Bay. God willing, we who live today never want to witness anything like it again. As long as ships sail the oceans of the world, there will always be some kind of disaster. Many brave seamen, of whatever nation, that make the sea their liveli- hood, through many strange and different ways, through fogs, gales, collisions and fires, will be in danger. So let us pray for 'those in peril on the sea.'

There have been many storms, but none so bad as the 10th February and many lives have been lost. After the storm Bridlington had a new lifeboat; in fact we got two. One was a gift to the town by a count. She was called the *Seagull* and she was a beautiful sea boat. Manned by twelve oarsmen and two coxswains. My uncle George Wallis was chief coxswain and in his lifetime he saved many lives. I remember years ago there was also the RNLI. All crews in those days were volunteers, and when there was a call for the lifeboat to go out to some vessel in distress, the coxswain would send up a maroon or a rocket, calling the fishermen to go to the boathouse. I have seen as many as a hundred fishermen clambering round the doors. When they were opened, there was a rush into the house. Those in front were pushed in by weight of numbers behind. Many a man fell and others jumped over him to get one of the lifebelts which hung on hooks. Men who did not get a belt crawled under the lifeboat carriage to grasp a bucket, and they were responsible for the lifeboat getting safely into the water. You would not think to see these men rushing for lifebelts and buckets that they knew that they were risking their lives.

While all this was going on, the corporation had sent the horses to pull the boat on the beach. There were eight horses to pull her through the streets. On the beach the men got into the boat and waited for the horses to pull her into the sea. These horses were trained for this work and they had to be up to their stomachs in the sea before the beachman, who were ashore with long ropes, made fast to the boat. When the coxswain thought she was far enough in the water, he gave a signal and the beach- man, with many willing helpers, pulled on the ropes and into the boiling sea she went. The oarsmen pulled with all their strength and main to get her through the breaking seas, and once again she was going on her errand of mercy.

On one of these launches a reporter was too near the carriage wheels when the horses started to pull her into the sea and a wheel went over the reporter and he was killed instantly.

On another occasion, a horseman was washed off his horse's back and was washed away and drowned. There were many anxious moments when launching the boat but the work had to go on.

In the same winter, a record launch was made. From receiving a distress signal to landing the crew, less than one hour elapsed. In that time the lifeboat had been hauled down to the beach, launched, sailed into the north bay and four men rescued. Ten minutes later the vessel called the *Onward* disappeared.

Early in the morning of 22nd December 1909, a vessel was seen drifting towards the beach. Her sails were in rags. The coxswain, who I must state here was my father's friend, and one of the five who won two medals with my father in the *Swiftsure*, when they rescued the crew of the *Victoria*, was without doubt one of the best and finest and bravest men ever to be in charge of the lifeboat. His name was Richard Purvis. He directed the launching from the north beach. The horses pulled madly into the sea and the boat went off the carriage on the first sea. Spectators held their breath as she was hidden from view by the tremendous seas, only to see her rise up to be safely on her way. It was difficult to get near the wreck owing to the high seas breaking round her. Two men from the lifeboat watched for their chance and made a leap on her deck, finding the crew exhausted after a long struggle to save their ship against the wind, seas and tide. They had battled all night and one by one they were passed to the lifeboat. Soon the lifeboat was on her homeward journey towards the harbour. A great cheer went up but the danger was not over. Huge waves were breaking at the harbour mouth and through that hell of breaking seas the lifeboat had to pass. A wave picked her up and turned her broadside, holding her there. Men ran on the pier to help those in the boat. Silence fell over the people on the shore but the coxswain shouted an order and swung over the tiller. The boat righted itself and rose to meet the next sea. Again she was spun round and lay on her side. Women ashore screamed "Will she ever rise?" Purvis gave another order. The crew were magni- ficent and pulled on their oars and got the boat safely into the harbour, with the crew they had risked their lives to save. Cheer upon cheer greeted those brave men.

This section has been lightly edited by Mike Wilson

The Storm

A poem composed by Sarah Ann Usher, aged 15 (date not known), to raise money for the families of the victims.

It was on the tenth of February,
A very lamentable day,
To old and young and every one
That dwelt at Bridlington Quay.

It was early in the morning,
Upon that dreadful day,
A little barge came bearing down,
And rolling in the bay.

The life-boat man'd with gallant crew
Of sailors brave and bold,
Went pulling through the boiling surf,
And through the biting cold.

A shout of praise is raised high
Above the raging blast,
She's reached the ship in safety,
And saved her crew at last.

They hasten with the shipwrecked crew
To bring them safe to shore,
And looking out to sea again
They see a many more.

Then these brave hearts and willing hands
Again put off to sea,
To save their brother sailors
From a grave so watery.

All praises to our life-boat men,
Who saved so many crews:
But listen while I tell you
Of more melancholy news.

The ships came running in so fast,
The men had hardly time,
With both the life-boats for to save,
Before the flowing tide.

As the day wore on, the storm increased
To a perfect hurricane,
When the ill-fated "Produce"
Behind the pier came.

Oh, it was a heart-rending scene
To watch the struggling men,
As two got into a little boat
And the sea swept over them.

It swept the boat from out their reach:
Oh, then their hearts would fail ;
They tried for to swim to shore,
But it was of no avail.

The black man, he swam manfully,
For life was very dear;
But something caught and broke his leg
Before he reached the pier.

Then these poor fellows one last look
They gave unto the shore,
They bowed their heads their death to meet
And sank to rise no more.

Their comrades crowding on the deck
Did loudly call for help,
But when help it could not reach them,
What must they then have felt.

They would feel that all was over,
And know their race was run;
They would humbly bow before their
God And say "thy will be done."

They would think of home and kindred,
That they ne'er would see again
And ask the Lord to grant that they
In heaven might meet again.

At last the time grew shorter,
And their last hour had come;
The ship that outlived many a storm
Now sunk beneath the foam.

The horrified spectators
Were horror stricken more,
As they turned their eyes from that awful
Unto the south side shore.

For the untiring life-boat men,
With gallant hearts and brave,
Were pulling through the chilling blast,
Upon the angry waves.

They were pulling up to southard,
To save some shipwrecked men,
But the ship sank e'er they reached it,
And she ne'er was seen again.

Then they steered to another,
To try to save some more,
And they saved the crews, yes, every one,
And brought them safe to shore.

Then came the brig, the "Delta,"
That lost so many lives,
That left so many orphans,
And many weeping wives.

The crew of the "Delta"
Then got onto their boat,
And left one old man in the ship
When they began to float.

But alas! A mighty rushing wave
Upset them very soon,
And sent them to the bottom,
To their everlasting doom.

Then nine brave men to save one crew,
Went pulling to the ship,
But one large wave came rolling round
And swept them in the deep.

And three were saved, while six were sent
To the bottom of the deep,
Without a minute's warning,
And left their friends to weep.

"Life-boat's upset, and six men drowned,"
The people all did cry,
With, many a throbbing, anxious heart,
And many a tearful eye.

The little town of Bridlington,
That always looks so fair,
Was plunged at once into a scene
Of death and deep despair.

And as the darkness did increase
The storm increased as well;
How many lives were lost that night,
No-one can ever tell.

For underneath the stone sea wall
A vessel there did roll,
And the breakers they washed over it,
And the stormy winds did howl.

They tried the apparatus,
But it was of no avail :
"Save us, save us, a rope, a rope,"
Was their last dying wail.

And many more were lost that night
How many is not known,
For many lights were seen to sink
Beneath the surging foam.

The morning came and with it brought
A fearful view to sight,
For on the beach were strewed about
The wrecks of that awful night.

And here and there dead bodies
Came washing to the shore,
Which had been full of health and strength
A few short days before.

It was a solemn sight to see,
Upon that funeral day,
As they lowered them down one by one,
In their last beds of clay.

That day will never be forgot
By many and many a score,
For great strong men did cry that day
Who never cried before.

Oh, may they raise a monument
To tell the sad, sad fate,
And teach us all to seek the
Lord Before it is too late.

For young and old upon that day,
They each and both did go,
They crossed the shining river,
Where the living waters flow.

And now they have reached that happy land
And are safe on the heavenly shore,
Where storms, and squalls, and tempests,
Will ne'er be known no more.

Appendix A

List of the dead – Bridlington

Harbinger   Richard Atkin
John Clappison
William Cobb
Robert Pickering
David Purdon James Watson

Margaret   Captain W Howard.
William Mills (aged 32)

Produce   Captain Wm Flisher (aged 44,
identified by Wm Court of Folkeston
who had a brother on same vessel)
Robert Court (mate)
Michael Gerald (is this 'the Negro'?)
Stephen Godden
James Fitzgerald John Redford

Arrow   Captain George Robson

Delta   Captain William Calvert
Richard Lindup (aged 19)
Simon Butterwick
Thomas Jameson
Caroline   James Maldon
Robert Newman
Alfred Sharman

John   Captain Stead Laraman
Henry Coleman
John Coleman

| Lavinia | Captain Anthony Hendson/Hindson? |
| | Thomas Thompson |

| Teresita | Captain William Sash |

| William Maitland | Martin Burke |

Ship unknown James Kellor (age 66) died at Flamborough

List of the dead – Elsewhere

Jabez	Mr George Lewis (master)
	George Green/Coleman (mate)
	James Burrows (seaman)

Terminus	Captain Samuel Edmunds
	James Reeve Mr Todd
	Two men (names unknown)

| Frankfort | Captain Belsey |

Appendix B

List of the survivors

Harbinger	Richard Bedlington
	Robert Hopper
	John Robinson
Agility	Captain Pringle
Bebside	Captain Sellers
Caroline	Captain Carter
Echo	Captain Davernish
Friends Increase	Captain Tabor
Margaret	Thomas Bacon
	James Lamb
	Walter Wallace
Peri	Captain Charles Cook
Rapid	Captain Hutchinson
Rebecca and Elizabeth	Captain William Dutton
Spinner	Captain Dodd
Urina	Captain Wright
Vivid	Captain Vary

**William
Maitland**   Captain Anthony Newton

Windsor   Captain Woodhouse

Worthy   Captain Frost

Yare   Captain Heard

Jabez   John Alger (seaman)
William Coleman (apprentice)

Mary   Captain Moore

**Admiral
Codrington**   Captain Wilmore

John Sells (mate)

Charles Langley (cook)

James Sinclair (seaman)

William Fullerton (seaman)

Launceston   Captain James Johnson,
32 Palmerston Street, South Shields

Francis Nock (steward),
13 Hardwick Street, South Shields

James Bell (mate),
2 Nelson Street, South Shields

Charles Bragg (boatswain),
7 Union Alley, South Shields

Robert Lorimer (carpenter),
Victoria Road, South Shields
James Fraser (seaman),
Union Alley, South Shields

Henry Pieper (seaman), 7 Wilson Street,
South Shields

Anders Backing (seaman),
East Holborn, South Shields

William Johnson (seaman),
16 Cambridge Street, South Shields

James Simpson (seaman),
50 Raglan Street, South Shields

George W Clark (seaman),
Pit Row, Tyne Dock

Anthony Craggs (seaman),
28 Grace Street, South Shields

John Mack (ordinary seaman),
10 Ropery Stairs, North Shields

George Edwin Scarle (apprentice)

Joseph Wilson (apprentice)

William Carr (apprentice)

Arctic Hero   Captain Dent
James Lee

British Queen   Captain C. Rowlands

Thomas Trueman George Liston

James Cowell (carpenter) Charles Bird

Thomas Allsopp James ?? (apprentice)

Henry   Captain William White

Appendix C

The Graves today

David Purdon – Priory Grounds
Died in Gale. Buried with
wife Harriet

Robert Pickering – Priory Grounds
Died in Gale

James Watson – Priory Grounds. Died in Gale.
Buried with wife Eliza, died 28th Feb 1871.

William Cobb – Two grave- stones, one in Priory Grounds, one in Bridlington Cemetery. Died in Gale. Interment is not in Priory records.

John Clappison – Died in Gale Grave at Sigglesthorne Church.

Richard Atkin – Priory Grounds – Buried under grass (plot 835). Died in Gale.

Christopher "Kit" Brown (lifeboatman) – Bridlington Cemetery.
Died 25th March 1898, aged 56. Buried with his wife Mary Ann.

John Waite Shores (photographer) Bridlington Cemetery.
Died 15th August 1910, aged 68. Buried with his wife Annie Maria.

Reverend Yarburgh G. Lloyd- Graeme Sewerby Church. Born 18th June
1813, died May 1890.

Richard Purvis (lifeboatman) Bridlington Cemetery – 28th June 1924 aged 73.
Buried with wife and son.

John Robinson (*Harbinger* survivor). Buried Priory Grounds, grave site
unknown. Died 15th February 1890.

Robert Hopper (*Harbinger* survivor). Bridlington Cemetery. Died 20th
August 1898.

Richard Bedlington (*Harbinger* survivor). Bridlington Cemetery.
Died 24th July 1900. In unmarked grave, classed as a fourth class grave
(Pauper's grave).

Hannah Purdon (David's first wife). Priory Grounds. Died 3rd July 1861
aged 28.

Count Batthyany died in 1906 in Stoke Dry, Uppingham,
Rutland, aged 77.

Appendix D

Vessels in the Gale

Name	Type	Home port	Location	Incident
Alpha	Schooner			Captain washed overboard
Baker		Sunderland		
Branch		Sunderland		
Clark		Sunderland		
Damietta		London	Hartlepool	Damaged after striking piers
Dolphin		Hartlepool		
Edward	Schooner			One crew member washed overboard
Euphemia	Brig		Cleethorpes	Leaking but saved
Fano		London		
Felix et Aimee		Nantes	Harwich	Captain Cordet lost
George	Brig	Whitby	Hartlepool	Loss of bulwarks and boats
Gibbs		Blyth		
Grocer	Shields	Scarboro'		Entered harbour leaking
Hero		Southampton		
Jane		Ipswich	Tynemouth	Loss of sails and leaking
Jessie		Hull		One man lost overboard
John Elliotson		Whitstable	Shields	Struck north side of harbour and grounded but later saved
Johns			Staithes	Loss of sails and bulwarks
Juno		Newcastle		
Just		Lagos		
Keen		Southampton		
Keer		Sunderland		
Kirton		Newcastle		
Lamb		Sunderland	Tyne	Stern completely stove in but reached harbour

Vessels in the Gale (Cont)

Name	Type	Home port	Location	Incident
Light & Sign	Schooner	Whitby	Shields	Assisted due to leaking
Lynass		Sunderland		
Madam				Captain's son, 18, and boat washed overboard
Maresdom			Scarboro'	Towed into harbour by two Filey fishing boats
Morley		London		
Nymphen		Blyth		
Orward		Seaham		
Preciosa		Lagos		
Reynolds		Seaham		Captain lost overboard
Richard and Elizabeth		Sunderland		
Sicily	Schooner		Cleethorpes	Leaking but saved
Thomas and Isabella			Shields	Grounded briefly
Trot		Seaham		
Ward		Sunderland		
Woodville		Seaham		

Appendix E

Lost at Bridlington

Name	Home port	Captain	Dead	Saved
Agility	North Shields	Pringle	0	6
Arrow	Sunderland	Robson	3	1
Bebside	Blyth	Sellers	0	4
Caroline	Yarmouth	Carter	3	2 Capt. & mate
Delta	Whitby	Calvert	5	0
Echo	Maldon	Davenish	0	6
Endeavour				
Friends Increase	London	Tabor	0	4
Imod	Hartlepool	Dobson	0	
John	Whitstable	Laraman	3	0
Lavinia	Seaham	Hindson	5	0
Margaret	Ipswich	Howard	2	3
Peri	Lynn	Cook	0	5
Produce	Folkestone	Flisher	6	0
Rapid	Whitby	Hutchinson	0	6
Rebecca & Elizabeth	Lowestoft	Dutton	0	4 or 6
Spencer	Blyth			
Spinner	Blyth	Dodd	0	
Spinney	Shields		0	6
Squirrel	Whitby	Peek	0	
Teresita	Harwich	Sash	6	0
Uranis	Worcester		0	
Urina	Middlesbrough	Wright	0	5
Vivid	Scarborough	Vary	0	4
William Maitland	Whitby	Newton	5	1
Windsor	Shields	Woodhouse	0	6
Worthy	Lynn	Frost	0	6 or 7
Yare	Lynn	Heard	0	2

Total 28 wrecks

**Total
44 dead**

Appendix F

Lost elsewhere

Name	Home port	Location	Dead	Saved
Admiral Codrington	Rochester	Shields		
Agabas	Saltfleet, Lincs			
Agincourt	Shields	Hartlepool		0
Alice			4*	
Ann	London	Mouth of Tyne		
Ann & Elizabeth	Fowey	Newcomb Sand	0	
Annie				
Benjamin Sarah		Saltfleet, Lincs		
Betsy Ann		Saltfleet, Lincs		
British Queen	London	Tynemouth		
Cyathia	London	Tynemouth		
Cynthia Ann	London	Shields	0	7
Czarina	Whitby	Nr the Coquet	0	
Defence	Port Mulgrave	Rawcliffe	0	
Donald Stuart	London			
Edward Jones	Waterford	Castletown Harbour		
Elizabeth Emma	Shoreham	Hartlepool		
Elizabeth Harrison	Hartlepool	Cleeness	0	7
Fanny	Hull	Cleeness		0
Fortune Teller		Spurn		
Frankfort	Seaham	Yarmouth	8	0
Harvest	Shields	Mouth of Tyne	0	
Henry	Withernsea			
Hood	W. Hartlepool	Hartlepool	0	3
Horta	S. Shields	Robin Hoods Bay	0	
Jabez	Whitby	Tynemouth	4	2
Jane Ann	Hartlepool	Middleton Beach, Hartlepool	0	8
Jane Eliotson	Whitstable	Mouth of Tyne		
Kate	Hull	Humber	0	
Launceston	S. Shields	Hasbro' Sands	0	16
Look Out	Grays			

* (Plus three who were sent to search for them)

Name	Home port	Location	Dead	Saved
Maria Elizabeth	Leith	Hartlepool		
Margaret Dandy		Cleeness	0	
Mary	N. Shields	Filey	0	4
Mary	Dieppe	Hartlepool		
Oronica	Scarborough	Shields	0	6
Patra	Yarmouth	Lido		
Peace	Yarmouth	Hartlepool	0	
Remembrance	Blyth	Mouth of Tyne	0	
Rose	Blyth	Tynemouth		
Stanley	Whitby	Hartlepool	0	8
Stranger	Tramore			
Surprise	Teignmouth	Yarmouth	0	6
*Terminus*Y	armouth	Hornsea	2	4
Thought	Lynn	Yarmouth		0
Treaty	Goole	Saltfleet, Lincs		
Two H's		Dunwich		0
Valiant	Jersey	NE Coast		
Vivid	Grimsby	Saltfleet, Lincs		
Zephyr	Hartlepool	Norfolk		0
Unknown		Humber		0
Unknown		Yarmouth		0
Unknown		Yarmouth		0
Total 53 wrecks			**Total 21+**	

Appendix G

The unidentified bodies and the inquests

Of the 25 bodies found on the Saturday, three were captains, and three were lifeboatmen, Purdon being one of them.

1. Henry Varley, sworn, said he found one of the bodies near to the South Pier, having a medal of the Shipwrecked Mariners Society, No 30298, also a paper relating to a ship named *Victoria*, and salvage money due to Captain Crawford, and a timetable of Seaham railway. The body was marked on the right arm TJT and a heart on the left with a tree.

2 and 3. Wednesday 19th April: Inquest held at Britannia Hotel on two bodies found that day close to the pier. One is identified as Robert Court, mate of the *Produce*. Shipwrecked Mariners Society Medal No 10579 was found on him. Verdict "drowned by shipwreck on the 10th February last." The second body was unknown. Verdict "Found drowned."

3 and 4. Two more bodies found during the morning on the south beach, with the inquests held at the Albion. Verdicts "found drowned."

5. Thursday 20th April: Another body found and inquest held at Albion. Verdict "found drowned." Total number of bodies found is now at 49.

6. The body of the negro of the *Produce* was later found on 11th February on the south beach by Mr Thomas Wathson and Edwin Wardell, and they remarked that he had nothing on but a guernsey and a flannel shirt. "A 'well-built Negro' who appears to have drowned while attempting to swim ashore."

7. Sunday 19th February: Body recovered near north pier.

8, 9 and 10. Monday 20th February: Three bodies found, two on north side around 40 years old, one on south shore. Inquest was held on Monday evening by Mr Jennings. One was the body of a boy, apparently not a seamen. Another, the man found on the north beach, was around 40 years old.

11, 12, 13, 14 and 15. Sunday 12th February: James Watson found, with at least four other bodies, two of them thought to belong to a fishing smack which sank at north pier. The other appeared to be around 16, well dressed, wearing Wellington boots, thought to have been a passenger. Snow was laying thick this day. Inquest held on 13th.

16. Monday 13th February: Richard Atkin found.

17. Wednesday 22nd February: Body of Robert Pickering found at Barmston in the evening.

18. On one body found at Fraisthorpe was a solid gold ring and a pocket book containing four sovereigns. This property was taken charge of by Mr Thomas Rounding. Joseph Turner was called to assist in removing the body. A medal was also found on the body, later identified as Anthony Hindson of the *Lavinia*, and his friends notified by telegraph.

19. The only one identified was that of Wm Mills of the *Margaret*. He had been starved to death in the rigging of his vessel.

20. In a book found on another body was the name Captain Hindson. This was the captain of the *Lavinia*.

21. Another man sported a tattoo on his arm representing a man and a woman with the initials WH and EH underneath. He was found starved in the rigging of his brig that was ashore on the south side around 9pm on Friday night.

22. Body with medal marked SMS No 13884, found also with a knife.

23, 24, 25, 26, 27, 28. On Saturday, at 2pm, an inquest was held on the bodies of David Purdon and three sailors, before Mr Wigmore, deputy coroner, at the Albion, and adjourned until a later hour, when it was held on eight more bodies. The ages of these victims ranged from 20 to 60. One of these bodies was the Negro (see number 6). None of the eight bodies were identified. Two bodies found at Auburn by PC Wallington, both between ages of 20 and 25. One had a society medal on the eldest No 29008; on the other a paper with Frimsbury, Kent, written on it. John Coulson said he was assisting PC Edward Wallington in putting the two bodies into a cart when four others washed ashore, two had also washed up at Fraisthorpe, upon one of whom he found a lock and a tobacco pouch, but nothing that would lead to identification. Dr Nelson said he was called in to see a body at Mr Appleby's at Wilsthorpe. It was evident that he had got out of the water alive but had died later. There were no marks on his body. The verdict on the nine men was "drowned."

29. William Cobb. Inquest held by Deputy Coroner W. Wigmore at the Albion Tavern. (See BFP 29th April).

Appendix H

The Fishermen's Monument

The four faces of the Fishermen's Monument in the Priory church-yard tell the whole tale of the Great Gale of 1871.

FORTY THREE BODIES
OF THOSE WHO ON THAT DAY
LOST THEIR LIVES, LIE IN THIS
CHURCH YARD

IN REMEMBRANCE OF
ROBERT PICKERING
JOHN CLAPPISON
RICHARD ATKIN
JAMES WATSON
DAVID FURDON
WILLIAM COBB
WHO LOST THEIR LIVES IN THE
HARBINGER LIFEBOAT
WHILST NOBLY ENDEAVOURING TO
SAVE THOSE WHOSE BODIES LIE
BELOW

ARROW ... SUNDERLAND
CAROLINE ... YARMOUTH
DELTA ... WHITBY
JOHN ... WHITSTABLE
LAVINIA ... SEAHAM
MARGARET ... IPSWICH
PRODUCE ... FOLKESTONE
TERESITA ... HARWICH
WILLIAM MAITLAND, WHITBY

IN LASTING MEMORY
OF
A GREAT COMPANY OF SEAMEN
WHO PERISHED IN THE FEARFUL
GALE
WHICH SWEPT OVER
BRIDLINGTON BAY,
ON FEBRUARY 10TH 1871

Appendix I

Wreckage found by Atlantis Exploration

I have always wanted to add a final piece to the Great Gale story by finding an item (or items!) of interest. I planned a diving expedition for August 2004, and managed to generate enough interest to have a team of four divers. However, weather and luck were not on my side, and neither was the cheap car to carry my kit either! Because it spent more time in the garage than on the road I used my friend's car. We got set up with one of the divers and then it started raining. We had to wait until it stopped before snorkelling off to see if the visibility had been affected. It had. It was so bad we couldn't see our hands in front of our faces. So diving that day was off too. Then one of the divers decided not to turn up (and didn't bother telling us!), and the other guy had been called back to work. As for my friend, he had a problem with his ears and therefore he couldn't dive either. So the ten- day expedition turned into a disaster!

However, I never gave up and kept going down onto the beach with a metal detector around the areas that have been illustrated in several paintings. The images must have been drawn from life so I matched them up with how the sea wall is today and began my search. I hit a target close to the wall but due to the tide I was forced to leave it and return later. Several times I have dug for this object and had my hands inside it at one point, which made me believe it may have been a pipe. After checking with the water companies I realised there were no pipes or outlets in the area and never have been. I later learned that it is a steel support for the wall itself.

On 21st June 2006, during another search, I dug my shovel into a pool of water to clean the sand off and accidentally flipped up a small black object. I took it away to clean up later, and it wasn't until the following day that I carefully chipped the encrusted object until it revealed a small piece of wood. By the time I had revealed the full object, I realised I had found a sailor's rigging knife, the blade long rusted away, but with the shiny rivet in the middle and four grooves for fingers.

After talking with several museums I realised there was no way to identify which ship it had come from, but I was confident it was from the Great Gale. Happy that I had found what I had set out to do, I handed over the artefact to the Harbour Museum in February 2007 for display. It was always my intention to have any finds on display so everyone could enjoy them and see my work. In my opinion, what is the point in making a discovery and nobody knowing?

After the Gale, wreckage was piled nine feet high.

Site on north beach where the fisherman's knife was found.

Epilogue

In June of 2009, I took it upon myself to honour the last survivor of the Harbinger, Richard Bedlington, with a gravestone to mark his last resting place.

After speaking to the local stone masons J. G. Gardiners, who work directly opposite Bridlington cemetery, they very kindly offered to do the memorial at half the price together with a generous amount from Bedlington's great-grand-daughter, Vivienne Buckley.

On 9th July the headstone was revealed to Mrs Buckley by myself and the moment captured for the local newspaper Bridlington Free Press, still going as strong today as it was in the days of the Great Gale.

This is the last resting place of a hero, and in my opinion not somewhere that should be forgotten.

I hope this book and the legacy of the heroes of 1871 ensure that this disaster is never forgotten.

The author with Vivienne Buckley, great-granddaughter of Richard Bedlington, at the unveiling of the gravestone July 2009.

Bibliography

The following publications have been more than useful in my research:

1.   *Dive Yorkshire* – Arthur Godfrey and Peter Lassey
2.   *Shipwrecks of the Yorkshire Coast* – Arthur Godfrey and Peter Lassey
3.   *The Plimsoll Line* – George Peters
4.   *Our Seamen: an appeal* – Samuel Plimsoll MP
5.   *Shipwrecks of the East Coast* (Volumes 1 and 2) – Ron Young
6.   *Full Fathom Five* – Mike Wilson
7.   *Shipwreck Index of the British Isles* – Richard and Bridget Larn
8.   *The Bridlington Lifeboat* – Fred Walkington
9.   *Fed Up to Top Attic* – Bette Vickers
10.   *The Great Gale of 1871* (local pamphlet) – Mike Wilson
11.   *The Plimsoll Sensation* – Nicolette Jones

Acknowledgements

Below is a list of people and organisations without whose help this book would not have been possible. If there is anyone I have missed out I apologise and thank you also.

Beverley Archives

Bridlington Library – Sarah Stocks and Alan Moir

Fred Walkington

Roy Leng – great Grandson of Leonard Mainprize

Ron Green – local author

Roger Brown – great grandson of Kit Brown

Middlesbrough Library

Ruth McDonald, curator of Bayle Museum

The Lord Feoffes

Robin Sharpe

Tony Ellis, Humber Coastguard

Jill Sanderson.

Cathy Goldthorpe

Chris Newall

Dr Katherine Webb, Archivist, York Hospitals NHS Trust.

Vivienne Anne Buckley

Guildhall Library

Mike and Diane Wilson

RNLI

Suffolk Central Library

North Shields Library

Lowestoft and East Suffolk Maritime Society

John Cooper, local artist

All staff at Bridlington Priory Church.

Mark Terrell

David Marchant, East Riding Museums Registrar

Beverley Archive

Bridlington Free Press

County Wexford Library

Essex Record office

Sunderland City Library

Whitby Archive Heritage Centre

Folkestone Library

Durham Clayport Library

Fred Walkington

Shipwrecked Mariners Society

Tony Ellis, Humber Coastguard

Adrian Vodden, Harbinger Arms Royal Humane Society

Leeds Central Library

Grimsby Central Library

Crimlisk Fisher Archives, Filey

York Library

ND - #0188 - 270225 - C17 - 203/127/6 - PB - 9781909544727 - Matt Lamination